James V. Lee

Escape

From

Korea

Major John J. Fischer, 1955

By
John J. Fischer

With
James V. Lee

Escape From Korea

ISBN: 0-9663870-6-6 PERFECTBOUND
ISBN: 0-9663870-5-8 CASEBOUND
Library of Congress Catalog Card Number 2003110798

PUBLISHED IN THE UNITED STATES BY SALADO PRESS, LLC

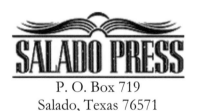

P. O. Box 719
Salado, Texas 76571

Cover photo by Squadron/Signal Publications (Digitally enhanced)

Contents

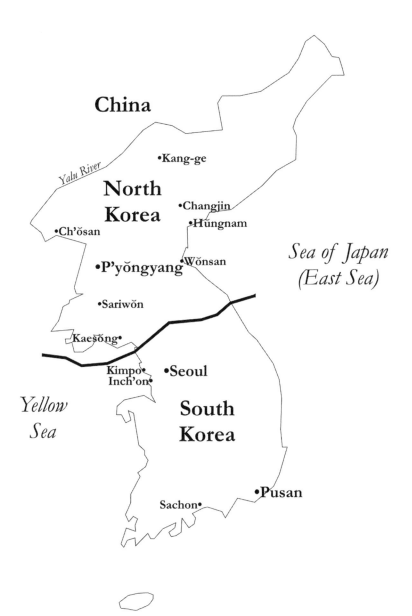

China

•Kang-ge

Yalu River

North
Korea

•Changjin
•Hŭngnam

•Ch'ŏsan

•P'yŏngyang •Wŏnsan

Sea of Japan
(East Sea)

•Sariwŏn

Kaesŏng•

Kimpo•
Inch'on•

•Seoul

South
Korea

Yellow
Sea

•Pusan

Sachon•

Prologue

Duringthe early weeks of June 1997, as we were in the turmoil of moving from Austin, Texas, to Georgetown, Texas, my wife discovered a dusty and disintegrating cardboard carton. It had been stored in our attic since I retired from active duty in the United States Marine Corps in the spring of 1963. It contained copies of some articles I had written over the years and a folder containing the rough notes I made during the Korean War, dealing with my collateral duties. One of these was to interview twenty-eight pilots of the United Nations who had been shot down behind enemy lines, had been rescued, and had returned to flying.

In addition, after several of the marine pilots who had been captured and held as prisoners of war were released in late 1953, I was given the opportunity to interview them and learn first hand of the events that led to their capture. These men also told me much of the North Korean Peoples Army (NKPA) treatment of POWs, and some tips on surviving in Korean and Chinese prison camps. Everyone I interviewed emphasized that the most important factor for evading capture until he could be rescued was a strong determination to avoid the one-a-day rice bowl diet of Korean POW camps.

Initially, this information was used to create an escape-and-evasion manual that was distributed to all squadrons. It was hoped that it might help other pilots unfortunate enough to become a victim of the results of a faltering airplane. In 1954, I submitted my escape and evasion treatise to the Department of Defense, but the war had ended and was considered best forgotten. My article entered the limbo of the Pentagon and was never heard from again.

After the fighting was over, my rough notes were stored away and forgotten, as was that mid-century war. In spite of my distaste for doing research, I finally organized the forty-eight-year-old writings, and transferred them to my word processor. Those writings, with encouragement from my wife of fifty-plus years and my three adult children, have evolved into this book.

Creating a book from past experiences began a strange mélange of torture mixed with bouts of joy. The torture came at two o'clock in the morning when many attempts to find the right words to paint a word picture of a situation failed to come forth. The joy came when, after the hundreds of painful hours, the book seemed to be completed.

The main character Capt. Gilbert X. Fox represents all the brave pilots who struggled through that unlikely war back in the dead center of the Twentieth Century. Many individual and compelling tales of mission, capture, escape, and survival were related to me during my time as a military pilot and debriefer. Fox's narrative is a true composite of these wartime accounts, as well as my own.

It is my fervent hope that the poignant experiences of the marine pilots who grace the pages of this book will enlighten and enrich the lives of those who read about them.

- John J. Fischer

Introduction
Coping with War

J ust the act of flying in the military can be a dangerous job, especially during a night carrier landing in rain and fog. When combat missions are added to the mix, casualties are a certainty and not all the casualties are on the battlefield. I was one of the lucky ones. I came back home relatively unscarred physically or emotionally. However, not all of my fellow airmen were so fortunate.

Although it has become more difficult to put names with those faces from a half century ago, the faces of my flying companions of the past are still vivid. One is that of the first marine pilot to be shot down and captured in Korea. He became almost the last prisoner of war to be released after the shooting stopped. The physical strain and trauma of a year in the POW camps left its mark. Some of the released POWs never fully regained their flying ability. Also engraved in my brain are the names of those friends who still rest in the red soil of that sad country. And only the Almighty knows the final destination of others who crashed during missions deep in enemy territory, or just disappeared.

I recall one marine friend, always a quiet, stoic man, who spent several months in the hospital undergoing treatment for his many ills. He was finally examined and certified fit for the actual control of aircraft in flight. Given his choice of duty after his release from the hospital, he chose to be trained in jet fighters and was sent to the transition unit flying F9F Panther jets.

A year after he returned from his captivity, his squadron was deployed to MCAS Mojave for gunnery exercises.

One morning while flying at twenty thousand feet above the desert, the marine radioed his flight leader that he felt ill and was returning to base. Five minutes after that call, his F9F Panther crashed into the desert near Mojave, California.

One of my best friends served out his commitment to the U. S. Marine Corps in 1953 and went to work flying for American Airlines. I was flying to Nashville to visit my daughter one day when I recognized the name of the airline captain. We spent two hours after the flight over beer and sausages. I got a message one sad morning that he had died suddenly of a stroke while on a layover in London.

Another pilot was discharged on some disability, the cause of which I never heard and never asked. He opened a flight school in Harlingen, Texas, and flew a Corsair for the Confederate Air Force unit in that small Texas town. In 1964, something went wrong with that now ancient Corsair he was flying at an air show at Burnet, Texas. He bailed out but struck the horizontal stabilizer and fell to the earth without pulling his ripcord.

There were other delayed casualties of a different sort. Not long after that war was beginning to fade from our memories, as wars are wont to do, there were occasions of sadness and feelings of loss when some good friends decided to end their marriages. Only a few divorces rippled through our ranks, but these seemed to have an effect on our unity. Those of us who had to face this latest storm didn't seem to know how to remain friends with either member of the shattered couple. My wife and I visited both, talked around everything important, avoided subjects we perceived to be painful, and went home unfulfilled. The "head" doctors told us these breaks were an almost natural result of the doubts and suspicions that often arise between husbands and wives after long enforced separations. Doctors always seem to have an easy explanation of tough problems, but casualties of war do not always bleed, and love does not always conquer all.

The event that changed the lives of all of us began on a rainy Sunday morning on June 25, 1950, when, without warning, the North Korean Peoples Army began firing artillery and mortar shells on the Republic of Korea Army positions south of the 38th Parallel, the line then serving as the border between the two countries.

- John J. Fischer

Chapter 1
Attacked

Within hours after the Secretary of State brought news that the North Korean Peoples Army (NKPA) had attacked the Republic of South Korea (ROK), United States President Harry Truman was in conference with members of the Security Council of the United Nations. Before the long day was over, they made a decision that would commit American armed forces to the Korean Peninsula.

Under the command of the United Nations, units of United States armed forces would be deployed to preserve the South Korean democratic government, and to halt the spread of Communism. These orders were sent to the various United States commands. Although the words employed the accepted diplomatic verbiage, they still meant war. Other UN member nations also issued orders and would soon join what was to become a multinational force fighting under the blue UN flag.

Fortunately for the Republic of Korea, the attack by the North Koreans began during the time the Soviet Union was boycotting the UN. The Soviet delegation had walked out because of some minor disagreement with the UN. Their absence prevented a veto of the Security Counsel's action, a vote that would have prevented any UN military engagement in Korea.

Shortly after news of the president's decision became known, there was frantic activity in the Dai Ichi building in Tokyo. Here, within the offices of the Far East Command, the staff of General Douglas MacArthur began to study the contents of "Contingency Plan ROK." This was a plan written to facilitate the deployment of elements of the United States' forces presently stationed in Japan to bolster the defense of South Korea.

The expectation was that the rapid deployment of these forces would accomplish a dual mission. They would be charged with the rescue of American civilians serving the diplomatic corps as well as the US Army Advisors (KMAAG) on the peninsula. The advisory forces and the ROK army troops were already in full retreat before the overwhelming NKPA surprise attack.

Upon his receipt of a "Warning Order" from the Commandant of the Marine Corps, the Assistant Chief of Staff, G-1 (Personnel), Second Marine Aircraft Wing at MCAS Cherry Point, North Carolina, spun the dial to the combination numbers that opened his office vault. He removed a red bound folder labeled "TOP SECRET," signed and dated an access sheet, and removed the "Contingency Plan (Korea)" from the folder. He spent the following four hours in a conference with the Commanding General, Second Marine Aircraft Wing along with the other members of the air wing staff.

One decision made during this conference was to send a cadre of Cherry Point marines to the West Coast to augment personnel of the First Marine Aircraft Wing. By 2200, the G-1 had compiled a list of twenty names of marine fighter pilots presently assigned to units of the Second Wing. These were marines stationed at MCAS Cherry Point, NC, and would comprise the first cadre of replacements for the First Marine Aircraft Wing.

The First Marine Aircraft Wing at MCAS El Toro, California, had already been ordered to duty with the United Nations Units and was in the process of deploying to the Korean Theater. Combat causes personnel losses, and the First Wing would probably need replacement pilots soon after it entered the fighting. The Second Air Wing at Cherry Point, NC, was the only immediate source of replacement pilots and ground support personnel until reserve units could be activated and trained. The list was in alphabetical order. My name Vincent X. Fox was third from the top.

The next morning each of the marines on the list was told to settle his affairs, pack his kit, and hold himself in readiness for immediate deployment to the Far East. The deployment would be for a period of fourteen months.

Two weeks later, the twenty arrived at Itami AFB on the outskirts of Osaka, Japan. I was then assigned to Marine Aircraft Group 33 as an assistant to the Air Group S-3 (Operations and Training). I served with MAG 33 in several capacities for five months. During that period, I was assigned the job of moving the forward echelon detachment of MAG 33 to Kimpo to prepare a facility for group air operations. This would require that I make the Inch'on landings with elements of the First Marine Division.

During this operation, I crawled up a ladder to the top of the stone seawall that prevented the waters of Flying Fish Channel from inundating the city during periods of high tide. I was met by a lot of highly motivated North Koreans doing all they could to discourage our entry onto Korean soil. When Kimpo Airfield was reported secure, I formed up a small motor convoy to move to that place. Upon our arrival, we made facilities ready to support the two squadrons of Corsairs and a squadron of Grumman "Tiger-cat" night fighters, the tactical units of MAG 33.

While MAG 33 was based at Kimpo Airfield, I flew many Corsair missions, escorting photo-recon flights from Kimpo Airfield to the farthest northern reaches of the Korean Peninsula. I also flew road reconnaissance missions (RECCE) that were designed to locate and to report enemy troop movements. Wing photo pilots ranged all the way from Kimpo to the Yalu River, the boundary between Korea and Manchuria, photographing the already snow-capped mountains and mapping the meager road and railway networks of North Korea.

During those cooling September days, I flew missions over the Chosin Reservoir and the mountains that dominated the central spine of North Korea. I recall hoping that we would never be called upon to fight in that rugged, forbidding terrain. I passed over towns with unfamiliar names like Kanggue, Hiesanjin, Chongjin, and the many unnamed villages that were nestled on the level places between those icy mountains. These were towns with which I would become all too familiar as the months passed.

Photo courtesy Lynn F. Williams, Col. USMC (Ret.).

Chapter 2
Navy Cruise

After I became a member of Marine Fighting Squadron 323 (VMF 323, the "Death Rattlers"), I was treated to life aboard a US Navy CVE (aircraft carrier—escort), sometimes referred to as a "Jeep Carrier," and often as "Henry Kaiser's Revenge."

The CVEs came into being back in the early months of World War II when Mr. Kaiser created a new concept of shipbuilding. By using his adaptation of production line techniques, his shipyards cranked out small cargo ships in amazing numbers with stunning rapidity, making an oversupply inevitable.

After the U. S. Navy Department decided the fleet faced a glut of the plodding cargo vessels, the planners decided to put a flight deck on these slow tubs and send them to sea with a few scout planes to escort ship convoys.

Even after they filled this objective, there were ships left over. Someone then remembered that the marines liked to have their planes close to where the ground troops were fighting. So why not send marine squadrons out on the CVEs? After all, marines always accept such tasks with gusto. Hadn't they attacked the agile Japanese Zeros with the slow, clumsy Brewster F3A Buffalos back at Midway Island? And hadn't the Cactus Air Force of Guadalcanal destroyed hundreds of Japanese airplanes with the inferior F4F Wildcat Fighter? The concept was considered viable and the ships were given to the marines.

So, in due course, the United States Marine Corps and the United States Navy gave me an all-expense-paid cruise aboard the good ship USS *Badoeng Strait* (CVE-116) in the exotic Yellow Sea. Here, they gave me the stimulating opportunity of dropping bombs on and firing guns and rockets at groups of Korean soldiers who always expressed their resentment of such treatment by shooting at our airplanes.

USS Badoeng Strait, underway on August 6th, 1952, while en route to the Far East for her third, and final, Korean War deployment. Seven F4U "Corsair" fighter bombers are spotted on the forward end of her flight deck. Photo courtesy of the Naval Institute Photographic Collection.

A mission began when I was strapped snugly into a ten-ton Corsair loaded with all the high explosives it could carry. A jolting catapult shot then flung this airplane into the sky. After an hour or so of dodging enemy fire, my mission ended with a thrilling, adrenaline-enhanced landing on the small, pitching flight deck. Darkness, foul weather, or a sputtering airplane that had suffered from the accuracy of some unseen machine gunner often made these landings more exciting.

Unless flight operations were in progress on the ship, the only lights after sunset were the dim red binnacle lamps on the bridge. This was standard navy operating procedure against submarine attack, however unlikely. A ship's captain would never be able to explain the loss of his ship while operating against a country that had no submarines. But North Korea had allies who did have submersibles and who could probably be coerced into sneaking in and sticking a torpedo or two into an American war vessel. Even if someone on the weather decks should thoughtlessly light a cigarette, the fire-glow could be seen for an amazing distance as a bright hole in the blackness of an ocean evening. Although the possibility of a submarine attack was almost non-existent, the "almost" word forced ships' captains to take all precautions against such an event.

Periodically, the ship was relieved of its combat duties and departed its sea station bound for its support base at Sasebo, Japan. As soon as the ship cleared the combat zone, we pilots launched our Corsairs, and flew a couple of hundred miles to the Itami AFB, which was situated a few miles from the Osaka-Kobe area and served as the home of the Rear Echelon Units of the First Marine Aircraft Wing.

At Itami, the service squadron mechanics worked to patch up bullet holes, to replace worn spark plugs, and to perform any other maintenance tasks on our Corsairs. While they worked, the pilots indulged in the luxury of long, hot baths, excellent food, and an unrestricted supply of whiskey at the Takaraska Hotel in the coolness of the mountains a few miles north of Itami.

Unlike some navies, the U. S. Navy has banned alcohol of any drinkable sort from its ships since revolutionary days. But some grizzled and thirsty veteran crewmember sometimes created a distillation device in the shaft alleys or other deep bowels of the ship where almost no one ever goes. Using dried fruits from the ship's supply, which he could usually barter from the cooks, he distilled an alcoholic concoction from prunes, apricots, or a mixture of whatever was available. The officer of the deck of one ship upon which I served during WWII, followed a strange odor and found a device that filtered Aqua-Velva aftershave lotion to render it drinkable. But otherwise, the navy expressly forbids exotic drinks or even the traditional grog on its ships.

Marine fighter pilots stationed aboard navy ships are known, even expected, to look upon this ban as one strictly for the sailors. When the ship arrived in a port, our landing signal officer, an ardent golfer, would go ashore to indulge his passion for the game and return with his golf bag filled with bottles of booze. Most of us kept a fifth of whiskey in the small wall safe provided in each stateroom and enjoyed an illegal nip before dinner.

After dinner, we often had time to indulge in whatever recreation we could devise. Since the business of a warship is to conduct war, entertainment of any kind rated a low priority. However, in these days predating television and VCRs, we did have a steady diet of old movies. Films were passed back and forth between ships of the task force whenever possible. Anyone who had been at sea for more than a month had seen most of the available films at least thrice.

Aboard the USS *Bennington* during the last months of WWII, the marines and ship's crew were treated to an action flick entitled *Lord of the Desert* six times in one month. By the third screening the audience had memorized the dialog and shouted their own version of the screenplay dialogue back at the actors, often using explicit words and phrases that would never pass even the most lax censorship. During those passionate love scenes between the brave White Hunter and the love-starved wife of the cowardly rich man, the projectionist would shut down the sound. The dialogue from the screen offered less entertainment than did the "live" performance of the ship's crew as they lip-synced their own words of passion. During the few days we were taking on supplies at Ulithi and after the third showing of *Lord of the Desert*, someone poured about a cubic yard of sand on the hangar deck where the movie screen was mounted.

Such was an evening of exotic entertainment on the high seas aboard a navy warship.

Chapter 3
Scut Work

I arrived at Itami AFB, Japan, back in the first days of August 1950, with orders to report to Marine Aircraft Group 33. At the MAG Headquarters, the Group S-1 (Personnel) assigned me to the S-3 (Operations) as one of three Assistant Operations Officers.

Captains who work in Group Operations, or for that matter in any job, spend most of their time answering telephones, carrying classified documents from one office to another, and doing any other scut work. The Group S-3, a lieutenant colonel, and his first assistant, a major, tell them what to do and when to do it. When I reported in, the S-3, Lt. Colonel Tom Ahern, gave me a large carton of jumbled files and told me to, "make some sense out of this mess."

A month earlier, just days after the North Koreans surged across the 38th parallel, I had been yanked from a very comfortable billet as an instructor pilot at MCAS Cherry Point, NC, and had begun my trip to Korea. I was a combat veteran of WWII, with hundreds of hours of experience in the F4U Corsair, and several hundred landings aboard aircraft carriers noted in my flight logbook. Because of this vast experience I had expected to be sent to a squadron where the Marine Corps could receive a benefit from all the money and time they had invested in me. My assignment to the staff job was less than a joyous occasion.

Then one week after I had arrived in Japan, just as I was finally getting all those mixed up files squared away and was finding my way around Osaka and Kobe, the "Death Rattlers" squadron had two of their pilots shot down during a troop support mission near Sachon, a small seacoast town near the southern end of the Pusan Perimeter defense line.

A flight of four Corsairs had been working with a forward air controller when an NKPA gunner got lucky. One of the pilots made a crash landing in the narrow bay. He was picked out of the water by a helicopter carrying Marine Brigadier General Craig to his Masan Headquarters. That pilot was wet and pissed off, but uninjured.

The other pilot was USMC Captain Viv Moses. His badly damaged Corsair was unable to make it to the relative safety of Sachon Bay and he was forced to crash-land in a rice paddy. Moses did the best he could but was knocked unconscious, and drowned in two feet of fetid rice-paddy water. The "Death Rattlers" were short of qualified flight leaders even before they lost Moses, so Major Arnold Lund, the squadron commander, sent a request to the Group S-1 asking for a replacement pilot.

I was the only warm body in the air group that satisfied the requirements, which included carrier qualification. So it came to pass the day before Labor Day, I flew an F4U-4 Corsair out of Itami AFB, Japan and headed west. As I passed over Itazuki at ten thousand feet, I began to receive a faint signal from the YE-ZB homing radio aboard the USS *Badoeng Strait*.

Forty minutes later I was over the ship, which had already turned into the wind. "Fly One" had hoisted the fox flag, and the landing signal officer was on his platform. I was on the downwind leg of the landing pattern, flying three hundred feet above the water, with speed ninety-five knots, wheels down, flaps down, and tail-hook extended.

My approach and landing was nothing to brag about. My two Field Carrier Landing Practice (FCLP) flights at Itami had demonstrated that I could probably get a plane aboard the ship without scaring everyone, but doing

FCLPs on a wide, stationary runway certainly isn't the same as landing on a small pitching deck.

The sea was a bit rough and the deck had what looked to be about a ten-foot pitch. CVEs can produce a pretty good deck pitch even in almost calm seas, so this was nothing out of the ordinary.

A CVE, even one just out of dry dock with a clean hull, is hard-pressed to generate the speed necessary to create much wind across the flight deck. After it has been at sea long enough to pick up a goodly coating of sea-growth, like barnacles and moss, it gets even slower. The *Badoeng Strait* had been out long enough and had lost several critical knots of speed.

F4U Corsair making a carrier landing. Photo courtesy Alan Abel, Aviation Heritage

Anyhow, after the LSO picked me up at the "90" with the standard "Roger" signal, he used every signal in the book, some of them twice, before I was more or less in the groove. I was a tad high, a little fast and somewhat overshot, but "Paddles" gave me a "cut" anyhow. I caught the number four wire, which ran out far enough to let me get a good close look at the barrier cables and the Corsairs that were parked on the forward flight deck.

After the landing, my Corsair, with me still strapped in the cockpit, was lowered to the hangar deck on the forward elevator. Beside the chores of securing the cockpit, the pilot had the job of following the commands of an unseen plane handler shouting for the application of brakes as the Corsair is squeezed into impossibly small areas among the other planes. After the shutdown, I completed the yellow sheet and climbed the ladder to the ready room.

The LSO caught up with me as I entered the room and, as was normal routine, gave me a critique of my approach and landing. This little talk is almost always a downer for pilots. After an aviator has made what he thought was a pretty damn good approach and landing, the LSO takes out his little notebook and uses his notes to deflate his ego.

In my case, he spent a full fifteen minutes enumerating the many faults of my approach and landing. He ended the tirade by telling me he didn't believe anyone could make so many mistakes during just one thirty-second approach. The only reason he didn't give me a wave-off and force me to make another approach was that the ship was on a course that was taking her toward water too shallow for safe operation. So I got what he called a controlled crash cut. He also called my approach and landing a "calisthenics approach," because all those signals had given him his aerobic exercise for the day.

Arnie had been watching my approach and landing from Fly One up on the bridge. He was a great hulk of a man who always spoke quietly but with purpose and confidence. He walked into the ready room as "Paddles" was ending his critique. We shook hands as he bade me welcome and told me that I was assigned to the Squadron Operations Department. We sat in the front row of ready room chairs from which we could see the map of Korea that was mounted on the wall. Major Lund spoke for a while about his philosophy of command and his knowledge of objectives of the ground war before we began that inevitable discussion of mutual friendships. That little talk included my being reminded of the fact that the marine I was replacing had been one of my students when I was an instructor pilot attached to VF-1 at Cecil Field back in 1946.

My assignment to the squadron operations began an era of almost sleepless nights. Ever since their arrival in the combat zone, the operations staff of the squadron had been hoping for someone with experience composing "After Action Reports." In desperation, they had decided that experience be damned. Whoever walked into the office next would be given that onerous task. I was it.

On a normal day, if there could ever be a normal day during that time and in that place, I could manage to hit the sack only after I had completed my collateral duty of compiling and dispatching those reports. This was usually about 2300.

All of the seemingly surplus paper work that is the result of directives from higher commands is a gross pain for combat marines. When a requirement for more paper work came down the line, it often aroused doubts about who the real enemy was.

Someone in a higher command had decreed that after every combat mission, whether there was enemy contact or not, all participating pilots would undergo a detailed debriefing. The people in the ship's CIC, the Combat Information Center, duly recorded the pilot's version of the flight, and the damage done to the enemy during that day's work. After the gentlemen of navy intelligence completed their analysis of the information, the rough reports were delivered by hand to our squadron operations office.

It was at this point that the day's debriefings were finally in my possession. My job was to put them into the prescribed narrative form. When I had finished this task, one copy would be placed in the squadron file cabinet. Other copies would be sent to the ship's captain, to the ship's communications center dispatch, to the Marine Aircraft Wing at Kimpo Airfield, and to the Fifth Air Force Headquarters at Taegu.

I don't think anyone ever gave these narratives more than a passing glance after which they were classified "SECRET," as if the enemy might discover that he had been bombed. The final move of this information was to be locked in a file cabinet somewhere in the headquarters building.

The transformation of the information gleaned from the pilots, through the hodgepodge of raw data into a form that gave a true account of the progress of the war, required a lot of time. After an initial collation, the data had to be composed into a form acceptable to the wizards at the Fifth Air Force and the Far East Command.

These higher, god-like commands had decreed that all combat reports be arranged in a specific order and couched in specific language, then typed onto a message form as a readable narrative. The form prescribed was precise and inviolate. It was as if people with limited vocabulary staffed higher commands.

The enemy equipment destroyed during the day's action had to be in the order prescribed: Enemy aircraft first, tanks second, trucks and artillery pieces next, and slain enemy soldiers last.

Sometimes in the dark silence of the night, I had a recurring nightmare that one of my reports came back to me in the hands of a blue clad Fifth Air Force "Staffie." He always wore thick horn-rimmed glasses, had a halo, and had corrected my work with abundant blue pencil marks.

The work was marked with the grade of "F" in red ink and had several caustic margin notes regarding my grammar and punctuation. The air force person looked a bit like my old high school English teacher.

Once the radio shack received the information for transmission to wherever it went, my evening's work was finished. Only after I had completed these chores could I go to the wardroom, talk the duty cook out of a sandwich created of cold ham or bologna, and retire for a night of restive sleep.

The rough "After-Action Reports and Analyses" were usually delivered to me about an hour after the last flight had landed. This time depended heavily upon two factors:

First was the elapsed time since their last meal, the intensity of the hunger pangs of the debriefing officers, and the dinner menu of the wardroom. More often than not, these men had been forced by their pressing duties to forego their lunch. Growling stomachs tend to overcome devotion to duty.

Second, delays in the delivery of the reports from CIC would be increased by temptations offered by that dinner menu. Carrier sailors rate fried fish, liver, and baked chicken as a number ten on the menu scale. But beef in any form, cooked in any fashion, even chipped and served on a shingle, always seems to rate closer to number one on the gastronomic scale.

If the wardroom menu included steak, roast beef, or even pork chops on any particular evening, the debriefers would decide that attendance at dinner had priority over the timely completion of their tasks. Besides, a latecomer on a steak night would often find that the allotted number of steaks had been consumed. The consolation prize was a slab of cold ham and some mushy, overcooked broccoli.

So the debriefers would decide to complete their work after they had enjoyed a steak or a slab of prime roast beef, and this action would cause the rough reports to be delivered to me much later than usual. By the time I had done my part and had sent the finished product to the higher commands, the choice food would be gone.

While the CIC people were enjoying a relaxing break from their duties, the dinner hours passed. Wardroom personnel would remove the tablecloths and cover the tables with green felt, then retire for the night leaving only a couple of mess attendants to see that the coffee urn was full and that late diners could get some sort of a snack.

All CVEs were cursed with a small food storage capacity and minimal refrigerator space. When the ship had extra mouths to feed, as when a squadron of two hundred always-hungry marines was on board, the CVE was noted for running short of foods, such as fresh meat and veggies, after only a couple of weeks at sea.

But even while the cooks still had a supply of the good fresh meat, the demand was often greater than the quantity prepared. The cooks planned meals and prepared food based on the average attendance at a meal. Because a meat entrée attracted even the most jaded appetites, these infrequent dinners always played to a full house. Officers who worked on the lower decks of the ship, those who usually decided the long climb up ladders wasn't worth the reward, were in the wardroom well before mealtime. He who came even ten minutes late ate ham.

At this time in my career, I had spent a considerable amount of time aboard navy ships. These ranged from troop transports with crowded living conditions requiring three sittings at every meal to larger attack carriers with spacious mess facilities, ample wardrooms, and plush accommodations even for junior officers. All of these seemed to be stocked with a huge supply of dried navy beans, which were served with ham and potatoes for breakfast on Monday mornings.

My third night aboard the USS *Badoeng Strait* was also my third evening of working too late for dinner to enjoy the published entrée, and thus was my third dinner of cold ham and soggy leftover French-fried potatoes. No one would ever be able to convince me that there wasn't some huge secret space somewhere deep in the bowels of this ship that was crammed with an inexhaustible store of cured, boneless hams.

Ships of the navy have always been replete with noises that challenge a night of deep slumber. A continual whine carried throughout the vessel as the various ventilating systems exchanged used air for fresh and the normal creaks and groans of metal plates strained against rivets and welded seams. Then that devilish screech of the boatswain's pipe further prevented sound sleep.

Shipboard life and navy tradition decree that the nautical lingo be strictly observed. The roof is the overhead, the floor is the deck, doors are passageways, stairways are ladders, and boatswain is pronounced "bosun."

So the bosun blows his pipe-shaped whistle over the ship's PA system, known as the 1MC, as a warning that the announcement that follows the shrill tone contains important information for all hands and demands that the crew pay heed. One common announcement made at every change of the watch is, "Sweepers, man your brooms, a clean sweep-down fore and aft."

Loading ordnance on F4U Corsairs, USS Badoeng Strait
Photo courtesy Naval Institute Photographic Collection

Chapter 4
The Flight Deck

Within the confines of the space assigned to the CIC are radar controls and monitors with sufficient communications equipment to allow any one to speak to others anywhere on the vessel. Of prime importance is the Flag Plot, which is an area of maps and situation boards depicting the surface and air conditions. The sailors who work there keep the captain informed. In short, the CIC collects all data necessary for the great ship to be effective in combat. But an aircraft carrier of the CVE class without its squadron is useless and almost defenseless. The soul of the vessel is the flight deck.

To the uninitiated, the flight deck was madness personified. During operations, the deck looked to be a jumble of men wearing "T" shirts of various colors. Each of the colors proclaimed to all the job of the wearer. People who wore red shirts usually handled things that either exploded or burned, and men wearing yellow did the things that sent airplanes off into the sky and stopped them short of disaster upon landing.

These men moved about the flight deck tending the needs of the airplanes. They tugged at gasoline hoses filled with volatile liquid to refuel the planes. They pushed small dollies loaded with explosive items such as bombs and rockets to be secured to the wing racks and shuffled wheel chocks and tie-downs to prevent any of their charges from falling over the side into the ocean.

This ballet was performed with extreme precision and safety amid windblasts from the whirling propellers of aircraft parked mere inches apart. The din of the flight deck precluded communication by any means other than hand signals with which these men created order from jumble as the aircraft were launched in a prescribed sequence. The total of sight, sound, and movement is impossible to describe.

Every aircraft carrier had a crew of sailors charged with the maintenance of the aircraft arresting gear cables, (the barriers that stop a runaway airplane) and the catapults that were able to accelerate a fully loaded plane from a standstill to flying speed in a distance of ninety feet. These sailors began testing their equipment at about 0100 in the morning when flight operations had been scheduled. This testing demanded the activation of the complete system of machinery with all its pumps and pressures. The barriers and the arresting cables were raised to their active positions across the flight deck. The cables were then drawn to assure proper tension that could stop a ten-ton airplane traveling at a hundred miles per hour.

Action began with a series of horrendous crashing, banging, and slithering noises that announced to those sleeping below that the morning tests had begun. The onset of that tremendous racket always blasted me, shaking and confused, into a state that hovered somewhere between sheer panic and drugged wakefulness. I had usually been in the sack about two hours when the din on the flight deck ended my sleep. It was caused by the clash of various pistons and cylinders that forced compressed air to operate the gear.

The work on the cable system began at this ungodly hour to assure the arresting gear was inspected, serviced, and operating properly before the first flight of the day was launched. Daily testing, along with any needed repairs, had to be completed before the aircraft handlers invaded the flight deck to begin their chore of "spotting" the deck with the aircraft needed for the day's operations. When the Corsairs had been parked in position for flight operations, the aft end of the deck with the arresting gear cables was covered with fully armed aircraft.

The squadron duty section marines were already up on the mess deck having their first breakfast. As soon as they had completed deck spotting, some of the more dedicated trenchermen returned for a second meal. Marines aboard ship live with a continuous prospect of being sent ashore to some airfield where cooked meals are non-existent, forcing them to live off combat rations and stored body fat.

As soon as the gear testing was finished, these marines began pushing, cursing, and towing F4U Corsairs about the hangar and flight decks, placing the right plane in the proper "spot" for the first launch. They muscled some planes onto the forward elevator and raised them from the hangar deck to the flight deck and then pushed them to their assigned spot and tied down.

The aircraft elevator would lift a "ready" Corsair from the hangar deck to the flight deck with a speed that amazed even old timers. As soon as the marines pushed that plane off the elevator surface, it would be loaded with one destined for the hangar deck. This process of switching twenty odd ten-ton airplanes from where they were to where they had to be in crowded conditions was completed in an amazingly short time.

After the Corsairs had been "spotted," the ordnance section began loading them with items of destruction. They lifted dollies of bombs, rockets, and ammunition belts to the flight deck on the bomb elevators. Then they pushed the dollies to the airplane and hoisted the ordinance to the bomb rack pylons and secured it into place. The six .50 caliber machine guns were fed with the necklaces of their belted fodder of varied ammunition, while HVARs, the high velocity aircraft rockets, were loaded onto the wing rails. Wings were unfolded to allow the testing of the rocket system to assure there was no stray voltage in the rails. A five-inch HVAR motor contained a solid propellant that could be ignited by a measly half volt of residual electricity, and thus fired, would scythe down anyone in its path on the flight deck.

The flight schedule for this morning called for two four-plane flights prebriefed to "Devastate Baker" for close air support. These planes were to report at first light.

Two planes of a second flight would check in with "Devastate Able," the Wing Tactical Air Control Center, pre-briefed for a road reconnaissance mission over the road network north of Seoul to Wonsan, to P'yŏngyang, and beyond. This mission was soon to be known as the "cannonball run."

"Devastate Baker" was Chris Lee's outfit that traveled with the First Marine Division and received requests for close air support from the grunts. Dev. Baker then called in Corsairs from the assigned flights to the job.

There was also a need for a two-plane CAP, a combat air patrol that would spend its fuel flying boring pot-bellied circles over the ship in deference to those admirals who still got hot flashes when they recalled the lack of vigilance at Pearl Harbor. Also, there were still many people around who remembered the damage inflicted on the carriers *Franklin* and *Bunker Hill* by single Kamikazes in the seas off Japan back in '45.

And all this could not be done until the deck crew had finished the testing at the expense of my sleep. This morning the squadron had eighteen of its normal complement of twenty-four Corsairs "in commission" and available for the day's work over Korea. Number 6 was on the hangar deck having an engine change. Two days earlier, Sam Richards had encountered a flock of migrating arctic geese as he recovered from a rocket run against a T-34 Tank just north of Osan.

A goose, when properly stuffed and basted for the holiday table, emits a delicious aroma, but after being over-cooked, guts, feet, feathers and all on the hot cylinders of an R-2800 Pratt-Whitney engine, stinks to the high heavens and makes the cockpit intolerable. Number 6 would be down for two more days and would then require ten hours of low powered break-in flight time before it could be included on the schedule.

Number 16 was still back at Itami where the Wing Service Squadron people were changing its right wing. Our skipper had been flying number 16 during a strike and was making a low strafing run on some trucks when one of his targets blew up so violently that he was forced to fly through a column of debris. Arnie barely made it back to the ship where it was discovered that the main spar of the wing was almost severed by a chunk of steel that resembled the frame of a Korean truck. Old number 16 became a "hangar queen" until the *Badoeng Strait* was next in port. It had been carried by barge up the Inland Sea from Sasebo to Kobe and them trucked to Itami. The new wing had arrived from the States, but number 16 wouldn't be ready for another couple of days, a moot point because there was no one to fly it out to the ship anyhow. It would remain at Itami until the *Badoeng Strait* made port at Sasebo and the squadron pilots completed their R and R and returned to the ship.

Numbers 13 and 22 were still listed on the Aircraft Status Board although both had been slowly settling in whatever ooze covered the bottom of the Yellow Sea. Capt. Blake and Lt. Rocco had been sent to shoot up a large troop concentration and had run afoul of some extremely heavy and accurate flak just south of P'yŏngyang where they both took some heavy hits. They had almost made it back to the good ship *"Bing-Ding,"* before bullet holes won out over engineering. When the last precious drops of oil leaked out of the sump, the engines seized, and they were forced to make side-by-side landings thirty miles from the ship in sixty fathoms of water.

Both pilots returned to the ship after a short helicopter jaunt, wet and mightily pissed. The air force pilots that were supposed to do some flak suppression for the Corsairs had arrived early. But discouraged by the volume of the flak, they had aborted their part of the mission before they had suppressed a damned thing and flew back home. When Blake and Rocco began their attack, they got clobbered. Captain Blake's flight in number 13 was the last Corsair to bear that number. Viv Moses had been flying a previous number 13, and two other 13s had brought squadron pilots to some form of grief after which the ship's captain decreed that the number be abolished from the aircraft inventory.

The planes remaining on the forward end of the flight deck overnight also required repositioning. Two Corsairs that were overdue for sparkplug changes were lowered to the hangar deck where the work would be done as soon as it was determined the planes weren't needed for the first sorties.

Two of the four "ready" planes were spotted on the catapults, the other two tied down nearby across from the CVEs island. All the rest would be pushed aft where the arresting cables crossed the deck, then parked and loaded with ordnance, ready for their pilots to fly them into harm's way.

I got the full benefit from the early morning noise as I slept in the top bunk in an aft stateroom directly under the flight deck. On a CVE everything is close to, just above, or immediately under something else. My stateroom was positioned so that I heard every thump, bang, bump, and screech as the arresting cables were raised and lowered. The first snap of the cables and the first bang of the cable risers woke me with a start. I never got used to that and could never get back to sleep once the noise began.

Anyhow, today the noise from the flight deck was of no consequence. Before my heart rate had returned to near normal from the sudden and violent awakening, the SDO, Squadron Duty Officer, opened the door to my cabin and turned on the overhead light.

For some reason, when Squadron Duty Officers find it necessary to awaken you, they either shine the searing beam of a six-cell flashlight into your face and/or turn on lights in the stateroom just to assure they have your complete attention and have utterly destroyed your ability to sleep.

The SDO has been up all night prowling the ship to check squadron spaces, the watch personnel, and the security of the airplanes. During his tenure, he has been drinking gallons of coffee and smoking dozens of cigarettes, and, by this time of morning, his intake of caffeine and nicotine and his lack of sleep have combined to give him an intense case of jittery nerves. These same conditions have uncovered and honed to an acute state all sadistic tendencies that may have heretofore been hidden deep in his psyche.

Arnie Lund demanded that people be kept fully abreast of the military situation. It was to comply with this that the SDO decided to awaken me with the news that my flight, originally scheduled for the mid-morning launch, had been changed and would be launched at 0530 on an extra mission that had been slipped into our day's schedule by Wing G-3. This was somewhat welcome news. It reduced the amount of time I would have to develop those pre-flight jitters that began when I arose and increased until the "cat shot" sent me into the air. The "jits" always faded away while I was on the way to the target, and remained hidden somewhere in my brain for the rest of the day. I could never figure that out. Maybe it was the thought of being on the catapult at the mercy of a bolus of compressed air while strapped in an airplane loaded with a thousand pounds of high explosives.

Anyhow, some time before midnight one of the VMF (N) 513 night fighters had spotted what he thought was a pretty large convoy of trucks moving east on the P'yŏngyang-Wŏnsan road. When the pilot spotted this convoy, he had already expended his ordnance, including his parachute flares. During his patrol earlier, he had spotted a truck convoy west of Hŭngnam. After several attacks, he had left them burning merrily in the night. He was on his way back to Itazuke AFB when he spotted this second convoy. He could do no more than radio the position of the enemy trucks. Then, when the night jockey tried to call someone to tell them of his find, one of those sunspot atmospherics screwed up radio transmissions and prevented him from reporting his discovery to anyone until after he had landed back at Itazuke AFB at 0030.

So we received an order to make a predawn launch to search the suspect area with the hope of finding the convoy and blowing it up before it could cause any mischief for UN Forces. The SDO said he would reawaken me at 0300 as if that would be necessary what with all the flight deck clamor only a few feet over my head. The pilots would be briefed for the mission at 0330, at which time we were to receive any late poop on the situation.

When the duty officer, true to his word, returned at 0300 to awaken me for the early briefing, I was already dressed and lying on my sack re-reading a Zane Grey Wild West Novel. In the story, a soft-spoken cowboy named Tex rode his white horse into a cowardly western town that was being dominated by a bunch of real bad guys who cheated at poker, insulted the town ladies, and wore dusty black hats. Tex finally convinced the cowed citizens to stand up to the leader of the bad guys, a gaudily dressed dude. At the showdown, Tex drew his silver, ivory handled six guns, and shot the bad dude. The event stiffened the spines of the citizens and the good guys won their town back. I really liked that part, which was standard in all Wild West novels. I hoped it would come to pass in Korea.

The racket from the flight deck had eased from bangs and crashes to the squeaky rumble of airplane tires rolling over the teakwood deck.

I am now and always have been an early riser. This obnoxious habit had me moving about before anyone was up and about, except the cooks, who weren't serving breakfast yet. The shower compartment is always empty in the early morning hours, and the coolness of the water helps me come alive, at least for the next few hours. Most of our pilots preferred to stay in the sack as long as they could in the morning, so they showered at night when everybody else did.

However, the evening crowd always got the shower compartment all steamy and musty smelling. The mirrors fogged over so you couldn't see yourself, and the place smelled damply of the many different soaps and aftershave lotions. The evening shower sessions also served to overload the ship's fresh-water system and to cause the water pressure to drop until the showerheads just dribbled their ration of water. This was a situation that never failed to bring down a warning that we were using too much fresh water, and, if continued, would cause us to be switched to salt water in the shower rooms.

The shaving was another story. Wartime photographs published in the daily newspapers invariably showed fighting men at the front lines wearing varying amounts of facial hair. If one does his patriotic duty by slogging through the mud and dust, beards were of no import. But for an aviator, a day's growth of stubble, even if it emerged as the semisoft fuzz such as mine, posed yet one more discomfort. On most close air-support missions, the flying is below ten thousand feet, and oxygen masks aren't needed. However, heat and stresses of the flight during a troop support mission below three thousand feet induces heavy sweat, especially during the turbulence of a windy day. Although it was not necessary, a cool drought of oxygen was like manna from heaven.

Unless a pilot had taken the time for his daily face scraping, the facial abrasion of wearing one of those smelly old WWII rubber oxygen masks, even for the few minutes of cooling bliss, was enough to get the full detriment of cheek chafing rawness that would last several days.

Chapter 5
The 0318 Breakfast

For the first few days after a CVE has been in port and has taken on a full load of provisions, the food is pretty good in freshness and variety. As the days at sea pass, this bounty soon decreases rapidly. We marines always sort of halfway kidded the swabbies of the ship's company about the food distribution. We claimed, usually to loud protests, that they kept the best chow for themselves and fed the beans and half-raw bacon to the squadron. I was never able to understand how a cook could fry bacon so that half of each rasher was burned, the other half raw. After two weeks at sea, the stores of fresh food had been diminished, and the food began to take on a less than thrilling sameness.

A plate of half-cooked navy beans for breakfast at three AM is not exactly a culinary delight. On Monday mornings, beans were the normal navy fare because the navy believed that all hands needed fiber and bulk to restore digestive integrity after a weekend ashore eating civilian food. At the normal breakfast hour, those beans would have had enough cooking time to be completely cooked. But the beans served to the early diners were a bit too crunchy, and the occasional bit of seasoning bacon too raw for my appetite.

My early morning breakfast usually consisted of one of those dinky little boxes of corn flakes doused in some reconstituted powdered milk, palatable if the milk is cold enough to numb your taste buds. There was also a plate of cold but rather brittle toast and some strawberry jam. The navy always served strawberry jam, never orange marmalade or fig preserves.

I would also have a glass of the juice of the day unless it happened to be prune juice or that battery acid the navy called grapefruit juice. A cup of strong coffee, ultra strong after enduring heat evaporation since it had been brewed last night for dinner (which I had missed), would top off my meal.

My 0300 appetite didn't take long to be satisfied. I wouldn't eat at all if not for that nagging thought that this might just be my last decent meal. When I finished eating, I took the stroll between the few Corsairs on the hangar deck and up the ladder to the aft ready room. At exactly 0330 the other three members of my flight dragged in.

Pilots rarely exhibit much enthusiasm for life at 0300. As a matter of fact, were it not for their shuffling movement and an occasional groan, pilots who had been awakened for the "early-early" could easily be mistaken for walking dead.

The aft Ready Room on a CVE was the larger of two Ready Rooms. When the first CVEs were sent out during the "Big War," they carried squadrons of Corsairs and TBM "Turkey" torpedo bombers, and each of the squadrons had its own Ready Room. Between wars, the aft Ready Rooms were air-conditioned and the "Turkey" squadrons were done away with. The forward Ready Room became an additional storage space to accommodate the extra supplies of clothing and equipment needed by the marines while they were away from their shore base.

A CVE Ready Room is a long narrow sort of a tunnel just under the deck edge. The main entrance to the room faces aft and is only a few feet from the exit that leads to the flight deck. A green chalkboard and a cork bulletin board flank either side of the door. On the left side of the entry, a Teletype machine with a print-screen stands ready to relay weather data and any other information to the pilots.

Whenever the Teletype is activated, a bell rings to call attention to the vital incoming message. The machine sometimes chatters but doesn't print, or prints things like "the quick brown dog," or "EOTAIN SHRIDLU" quietly and without clatter. On rare occasions, some unknown sailor, alone in the CIC or at some other terminal of the Teletype and having no chance of being apprehended, will send a message requesting the admiral to perform an unnatural act on himself.

Since my first cruise on a CVE, the ship's crew always had at least one sailor with a distorted sense of humor, and lots of time to conjure up different forms of devilment. This swabbie humorist might manifest his mischief in several ways. On the *Badoeng Strait*, he messed with the ready room Teletype, sending his usually obscene messages to the admiral.

Aircraft carrier ready room. Photo courtesy John J. Fischer.

Down each side of a center aisle in the Ready Room were rows of upholstered leather chairs, enough to accommodate all the squadron pilots and some of the occasional visitors. Each chair was equipped with a foldaway arm that looked like the writing arm of an old student's grade school chair. One side of the room had four chairs abreast, the other two.

These chairs were obviously designed by a pilot who spent a lot of time sleeping in these rooms or playing Acey-Deucy because they are without a doubt the most comfortable chairs on the ship. Rumor has it that during the time of the big squadrons in World War II, an ensign from the ship's company put on a flight suit, slipped into the Ready Room of the fighter squadron, and remained there, leaving his sanctuary only for meals, for an entire deployment.

He was the Ensign Pulver of the ship. He never was missed from his regular duties, never stood duty watches, and never was noticed during the flurry of activity that preceded a combat launch. Neither the squadron CO nor the pilots who spoke to him daily ever noticed that the ensign never did anything other than eat during meal times and sleep in the Ready Room.

At this time of day the space was sparsely occupied. The only occupants of the Ready Room were the SDO, his corporal of the guard, and two squadron pilots who, finding their usual quarters too hot for restful sleep, had passed the night in the Ready Room, sleeping in the soft chairs and enjoying the air-conditioned coolness.

Chapter 6
Pilot Briefing

The flight this morning would be my twenty-fifth mission against the NKPA. After you have listened to the words of briefing officers twenty or more times, you begin to get the idea that the briefings are a necessary study in futility. However, a proper briefing imparts a lot of information that can be a huge help toward survival.

The weather, of course, seems to take precedence. One can always use his experience and instincts to evade danger when the enemy tracer-bullet pattern flies thick over the target. But if he nods through the weather section of a briefing, and misses out on the fact that a heavy fog is moving in, he can lead his flight into one of those rock-lined clouds and thus enter the rolls of those missing in action.

All the briefing officers are highly qualified, intelligent, and dedicated men who wish they were in a squadron, flying combat missions. They have at their disposal the most up-to-date information about the weather, the enemy and his dispositions, and have spent extensive time refining and condensing this information.

The bug-a-boo in all this is the time factor. The "latest" available information about the enemy can be old by many hours, perhaps even days, for many reasons. Ongoing ground combat situations were continually changing as both sides altered the deployment of units. Pilots flying over the battlefield on troop-support missions saw only a small segment of the action. What they had seen would often change radically during the time it took for the pilots to return to their bases, be debriefed, and have the "latest" information relayed to the officers briefing a later flight to the same target.

Information received through the normal communications networks, even messages classified as "Operational Immediate," experienced some delay that reduced the accuracy of an ever-changing battle situation.

Since the days of their initial successes and the advent of UN air strength, the North Koreans had learned to make full use of both the long nights and the opportunities of bad weather, which allowed them to move troops and weapons without being seen. Thus, the reports we received from the previous night's observations had become obsolete the next morning.

As always, some error resulted from completely inaccurate pilot reports, which were tainted and enhanced by the adrenaline of combat-induced emotion, and rarely, with some pilots' desire for medals.

A long standing proof that pilots sometimes tend to exaggerate came during the first months of WWII when Japanese pilots reported the "confirmed" sinking of the aircraft carrier USS *Lexington*, which survived that conflict better than did the Japanese. Some others reported the positive destruction of targets that seemed to recover from their demise in time to wreak havoc on ground troops mere hours after such destruction.

The big problem was that the briefing officer gave out all the stuff he deemed vital to the pilot. He told of the weather over the target area, the latest known placement of heavy AA guns, and the last reported positions of friendly ground troops. All of this was good to know, but by the time reported, the data had often radically changed.

During his briefing, a pilot was given on a small sheet of paper the verification and authentication codes that were valid for only the next four hours. These codes were used to foil any enemy attempts to divert or abort an air mission by the use of a sort of password and reply to radio transmissions. Although I hadn't heard of the NKPA attempting such subterfuges, they were so common during WWII that the ground marines employed "Code Talkers," Navajo Indians using their native tongue to transmit orders.

During that conflict, I flew close to two hundred missions and was called upon to use one of these codes only once. When I finally found my issued code slip under all the navigation data I had scrawled on my kneeboard, checked the querying letters, and answered the challenge, I got it wrong. The Air Control Officer refused to accept my bungled authentication, after which I blasted him with a rather unique and profane transmission that convinced him I was who I said I was.

After the detailed general briefing, I took my pilots Buck, Snick, and Jordan back to the ready room where we studied our own maps, set our route to the target, and went through a sketchy review of our own in-flight procedures. Every squadron has SOP, standing operating procedures, and each flight has developed some SOP of its own. This short private briefing consisted of our deciding on a "chatter channel," a radio frequency we could use when we didn't want anyone to listen, and a few minutes for a refresher on our flight SOP.

Although these are things that we discussed almost daily, and were procedures that squadron pilots used during every training flight they flew before this war even got started, these were important automatic responses in an emergency.

There were a few minutes after the briefings for the pilots to attend to whatever personal things they deemed necessary. First, each pilot went up on the flight deck to preflight his assigned aircraft. The plane captains did an outstanding job, but with all the pushing and shoving of aircraft in close quarters, it was always possible that some-one had "dinged" your plane, bent a trim tab or nicked a propeller blade. Whoever did the deed wouldn't be the one who busted his ass when the "Cat" slung that plane into the air. At this phase of my life I had already lived longer that I ever expected to and had come to like the thought of longevity.

Back in the Ready Room, you removed anything that might be of help to the enemy should you come to some form of grief and end up as a POW awaiting exchange. You retained only your dog tags. Then you checked your pistol, and copied all the latest navigation data, such as any changes in radio frequencies and the latest Point X-Ray. That was where the ship intended to be when you re-turned. And finding it easily when your Pratt-Whitney was running on fumes was vital. After you were sure you had all the necessary dope, you would take a few seconds to arrange your kneeboard so you can find what you needed when you needed it.

Just as we were beginning to break up from "talking the mission," the ship's air officer walked into the Ready Room and handed me a slip of paper containing the latest reported information on an air force P-80 pilot who took some barbs and had been forced to eject from his burning Shooting Star. This happened ten miles east of Kaesong the previous evening just before darkness made search impossible. The other members of his flight had seen his parachute open but hadn't seen him on the ground be-cause of the gathering night and about five-tenths cumulus cloud coverage.

On our way to our target, we were ordered to fly over that area for a quick look. I decided that, barring any un-tenable AA, we would cross the terrain low to get a good look. We had the coordinates of the P-80 crash and would try to locate the remains of the airplane. If we had fuel and time after completing our assigned mission, we could do some searching on our way back to the ship. If we spotted the downed pilot, we would get a good fix on his position and relay the information to the amphibious command ship near Inch'on. On our return, fuel allowing, we could even fly some RESCAP, rescue combat air patrol, over the area.

After our briefing, we all walked to the nearest "head" and nervously relieved ourselves. The Ready Room Teletype clattered an affirmation of our assigned airplane numbers and their locations on the flight deck.

The aft end of the deck was filled with airplanes, making a deck launch impossible, so the Corsairs assigned to Buck and me were strapped onto the catapults ready to go. Snick and Jordan were just aft of the "Cats" and would be loaded and slung into the air after we were clear of the machines and on our way.

Our flight used a pretty standard after-launch procedure, so we had no need for more than a mention of our join-up after launch. Since our two planes would be launched within seconds of each other, Buck would join on my wing, and we would fly in a slow climb on course at reduced power until Snick brought his two planes of the flight into position. The elapsed time between the four "Cat" shots was amazingly short, so the second section of the flight could catch us without wasting fuel in 180-degree rendezvous flying.

I set a course that would take us to landfall around the Haeju-Onjin area. Navigating wasn't a problem. The ship was operating just fifty nautical miles from the Korean Coast so I would head east. There was no way we could miss the Korean Peninsula because the coastline had so many distinctive landmarks. The wind was almost calm from the west, and the visibility was good enough that I would be able to make course adjustments before we made landfall.

The Teletype was sitting in its corner making its usual sporadic non-comments. Someone in CIC typed in the longitude and latitude of the ship's position, or what the ship's position was at 0430, and the present course and speed, as if we gave a tinker's damn. When we launched from a carrier in mid-Pacific, these things were more important. However, here in the confines of the Yellow Sea, if the weather was clear with decent visibility, we could merely call for a steer to the boat. In any event, we could always tune in the ship's homing radio and fly home. Latitude and longitude were for the multi-motored Pogues who could pass pertinent navigation information back to their navigator and wait for that stalwart to perform his math and then tell the pilot what course to steer.

Just as I was beginning to doze off for an early catnap, the bells rang and the Teletype began its clatter. The message on the yellow screen got as far along as "PIL," when the Ready Room speaker boomed out the order, "Pilots man your planes!"

Pilots scrambling for their planes. Photo courtesy John J. Fischer.

Chapter 7
Mission of No Return

This was the time when everything seemed to be in a state of panic. While there was an air of calmness in the Ready Room, when the order came down to "man your planes," chaos soon took over. The flight deck was a sea of deliberate activity, but the pilots rushing about amongst the parked planes were the only people that were in any rush to get somewhere.

It also seemed to me that it took a lot of time to move out of the Ready Room, down a short passageway and to climb the four-foot ladder to the flight deck. To thread your way among the Corsairs while your eyes adapted to the darkness meant bumping into several varied and sharp objects. Propellers were the main objects of my clumsiness, with deck-pad eyes and tie-down cables running a close second.

The run to the airplane and the climb into the Corsair cockpit from the flight deck with all my combat gear always left me panting and sweaty. I believed this time and physical exertion was specifically designed by the navy to replace the pre-combat jitters with the immediacy and stress of pre-flight preparation. The concept worked beautifully.

The elapsed time from the order to "man your planes" until the catapult slung your plane into the air was about ten minutes. These were minutes crammed with urgent activity.

The first task was storing and securing all gear. The navigation chart board had to be guided into its slot and latched securely in place. Next came the fastening of the parachute straps and seat harness, each adjusted for snug fit. When the Corsair was securely fastened to the pilot's butt, it was time to plug in the "G" suit hose, radio connector wires, and oxygen masks, in the event oxygen was needed. Then came the prestart cockpit check. The master power switch was flicked to "ON" and, as the radios came to life, the pilot could "press to test" various warning lights.

The sudden acceleration of a catapult shot will cause all loose objects to move abruptly to the rear of the cockpit or into the front side of the pilot, whichever comes first, so a quick recheck for any loose gear was always advisable.

These prelaunch tasks were performed with deliberate haste. Everything had to be completed before the "fly one" boomed out with the orders to "stand clear of propellers." This order was followed almost immediately by, "Prepare to start engines," which involves a flurry of flipping switches, setting fuel valves and circuit breakers, and flicking engine primers. Then came the final, "pilots start your engines!"

As the blue-white smoke of the engine starts cleared the flight deck, the ship turned into the wind. CVEs heeled over when they turned and made you feel as if you were going to fall off the flight deck into the sea.

Four two-thousand horsepower R-2800 Pratt-Whitney radial engines make a lot of noise, even before the pilots advance throttles to thirty inches of manifold pressure to check magnetos. This is accomplished by switching the ignition switch to left, back to both, to right, and again back to both while watching the tachometer. It is also the time to assure the engine is producing full power. It should show 2300 rpms at 30 inches of mp.

The old air-driven catapults were designed to accelerate the twelve-ton, fully loaded Corsair from zero to ninety knots within ninety feet. The main disadvantage of the air catapult was that it produced the most power as soon as it was activated. This gave the pilot a big kick at the start of the ninety-foot run, after which its power tapered off.

The Corsair had a small metal retractable rod mounted in front of the throttle quadrant. This handle would allow the pilot to grip the throttle with his thumb while clasping his fingers around the grip to make sure he kept full power during the sudden acceleration.

When the catapult crew had the plane secured on the "Cat," the catapult officer would signal for the pilot to "rev" his engine to full power. When all engine gauge needles were in the "green," the pilot put his head firmly against the headrest and saluted the "Cat" officer that he was ready. With that salute, a pilot placed his fate into the hands of the "Cat" officer and the machinery.

And with that salute, it became too late to alter any future events. If the pilot wasn't completely prepared to suffer the "shot," it made no difference. Split seconds after he had saluted the officer the catapult was fired. Tons of compressed air sent his aircraft down the deck and into the air. If he wasn't properly braced for this, he was slammed back into his seat, creating unintended consequences. The throttle might back off to idle, and any unsecured items, including the pilot's arms and legs, would move abruptly to the back of the cockpit.

The secondary fault of the air-driven catapult was that there were occasions when a plane got what was referred to as a "cold shot." In a "cold shot" the catapult gave only enough push to start the plane down toward the end of the deck. The plane never got near flying speed and sort of dribbled off the end of the flight deck. A lucky pilot got a swim in the sea; the less-than-lucky suffered the experience of sitting amid several thousand pounds of exploding ordnance and aviation fuel.

One of the pilots in another squadron had suffered this indignity back in '48. He survived the flames of his burning fuel tank only to have been struck in the crotch by the USS *Midway Island*, which was traveling at almost twenty knots. He reported back aboard, bruised, aching, and with a severely swollen scrotum. His condition required his evacuation when the ship reached port at Gibraltar.

That first big kick, the velocity of the wind across the flight deck, plus the full power of the Pratt-Whitney R-2800 two-thousand-horsepower engine usually got you into the air before you had time to screw up with the controls and hurt yourself.

The "Cat" officer was standing off my right wing as I saluted that I was ready. Then, with his whirling flashlight pointing toward the bow, he disappeared, as did the ship and everything that had tied me to Mother Earth.

I was flying into a darkness that was just beginning to show pink streaks of another day. Buck slid into position on my right wing thirty seconds later. Snick and Jordan joined in the "finger four" formation as we were climbing through three thousand feet. The sea was mostly devoid of ships although there were several fishing boats with their kerosene lanterns glowing off to our right.

Test guns. We switched on our master-arming switch and each pilot fired a short burst into the darkness and watched his tracers drop toward the black sea.

"Feet dry." It always seemed to me that the carrier was deeply concerned that pilots get over land as soon as possible, and that they report that fact to the Combat Information Center. I suppose that if a plane went down in the sea, it caused a lot of trouble and some extra paper work. On the other hand, going down over land put the rescue chores under the responsibility of a different command. At any rate, it was always vital to report when you were over dry land. To confuse the enemy, the radio code used to report this momentous occasion was a terse, "Feet dry." I'm sure that carefully coded phrase really confused our enemy.

One day "Big Sam" reported his arrival over dirt by stating that his "pecker was dry." Except for the fact that some deep-water battleship admiral was listening in on the tactical net, Sam would have gotten away with this "blatant lack of radio discipline." As it was, Sam was ordered to write an explanation of his sinful behavior and send it up the chain of command. General Harris received the letter, was told of the incident, and threw the missive into his burn basket.

We made landfall at Yonan. Once over land, we began our search for any sign of the downed air force jock. At Kaeson, a few black blossoms of anti-aircraft fire bade us good morning but gave us nothing to worry about. We saw no sign of the downed pilot, so we flew past the area to the Imjin River, turned north and crossed the 38th parallel between the Imjin and the Wonsan-Seoul Railroad.

It was soon obvious that the night fighter was right about the truck convoy but mistaken about the location. We could see evidence that many trucks had been driven off the Sariwon to Kumhwa Highway, and had tried to hide themselves in the trees growing along the bed of the Yesong River. We began our work immediately.

The trucks that survived the night had been driven deep into the forest in an attempt to hide from an attack they knew would certainly come at first light. There were several Koreans out in the open using tree branches in an attempt to erase the giveaway trail from the road to the trees. I recalled a western movie where some cowboys used the same tactic to erase the hoof-prints of their horses to evade the Indians. These NKPA soldiers sensed what was about to happen to their trucks and friends as soon as they saw our planes turn toward the grove of trees. None of them moved toward the forest in an attempt to hide from us. They just stopped what they were doing and dropped to the ground.

I radioed the flight of my intentions, and then flew by the woods low enough to allow me to look under the canopy of the trees. The trucks were about fifty feet in from the edge of the trees. The NKPA drivers had cut other branches and piled them around their vehicles to camouflage their presence. I could see the flashes of rifle fire from the woods.

I fishtailed to signal the flight to drop into trail and circled to the right until I crossed the Yesong. When I began my first run, some NKPA guy sitting on a nearby hilltop finally realized the convoy had been spotted and began to fire at us with a small caliber automatic weapon. The tracers from his weapon were falling way short, so I kissed him off as being no threat.

As I passed over the edge of the small forest, I pickled my "Nape" tank. The tank burst in the treetops and exploded, spreading its bolus of hot greasy fire down among the trucks. Buck's Napalm didn't ignite. It struck the ground having somehow missed the larger tree branches, then broke apart and spread its soapy flammable mixture among the trucks and people.

Snick was far enough behind Buck to avoid flying through the flames, so when he saw Buck's dud hit, he snapped a few rounds from his fifties into the general area. The tracers lit off the scattered napalm. Soldiers dropped from want of air, and more trucks began to burn.

Just as Jordan dropped his tank, something in the holocaust blew like the Hiroshima cloud. Jordan, who was forced to fly through the fire and smoke, made a comment about always being Tail-Ass Charlie and getting to fly through all the exploding crap and corruption but reported that there seemed to be no undamaged trucks under the smoke and fire we had created. What had been a quiet grove of trees was rapidly becoming an inferno of destruction.

After that first run and the good hits by the four one-hundred-fifty gallon Napalm tanks, there didn't seem any reason to continue beating that dead horse. The flight had been given a secondary mission of seeking targets of opportunity. We still had our HVAR's and full guns and plenty of fuel, so I turned north to hunt for something on which to expend our remaining ordnance. If we couldn't find a military target, we would be forced to dump our stuff into the sea before we would be allowed to land. Dumping perfectly good ordnance on innocent sea creatures was a waste of effort.

The squadron had learned to avoid P'yŏngyang the hard way. Flak sites surrounded that city, and the gunners were pretty good. This fact had been demonstrated two days before I joined the squadron when Pat Milkin had been hit just east of that capital city and couldn't run fast enough to escape capture. We could see no reason to get the North Koreans more pissed off than they already were, so I led the flight to the east of that beehive city. A railroad and a highway ran through Yongdok, affording a good chance that we could find some kind of military target.

The trip was mostly futile. Buck saw a single truck and went down to give it a pop, when I noticed something I really didn't like. There behind some rocks on the top of a hill that overlooked the road, was an automatic weapon, winking and blinking at us as we traversed the area.

Chapter 8
Shot Down

N ow one directive comes to the fore that I have always preached and preached to younger, inexperienced pilots I may have in my charge. It's often referred to as the Eleventh Commandment of pilots flying troop air support missions. The commandment is "THOU SHALT NOT DUEL WITH ANY GUN THAT MAY BE SHOOTING AT YOU."

No matter the irritation, no matter the distraction, no matter anything, do not get into a pissing contest with that fellow. The trade-off just isn't worth it. When you begin to run in toward the ground gun, you give the shooter a straight shot at your plane. Sure as a barnyard stinks, some little enemy gunner who doesn't know beans about shooting at a moving target will get lucky and put a couple of darts into you, your engine, its oil coolers, between your ears, or all of the above, and you will find yourself either dead or beginning a long walk home after having gambled an expensive Corsair against the life of some North Korean teenager, and lost the bet.

But it's early in the morning. Today I have already endured a pre-dawn launch and a successful attack against the enemy. Now I am flying over enemy territory with two hours of fuel in my tank, a full load of ammo in the gun pans, eight deadly five-inch rockets on the wing rails, and no other targets in sight. This is a set of conditions that will tempt one to ignore that "Do Not Gun Duel" commandment.

To return to the ship would require jettisoning the perfectly good ordnance into the sea. So in an attempt to give the American taxpayer a full return on his investment, pilots will frequently attack insignificant targets, such as some guy popping at him with a small machine gun.

In less than three minutes, I had won the duel by putting a few rounds from my six .50-caliber machine guns into the rocky hilltop the gunner had chosen for his fighting hole. Buck was keeping an eye on me while he searched around the hills for more enemy soldiers. As I pulled out of my dive on the machine gunner, Buck came on the radio to warn me of another weapon that had begun popping at me from another hilltop across the narrow valley from the first.

This second guy was either lucky or more skillful. I had spotted the muzzle flash from his machine gun and was turning toward his position, when I heard that frightening sound of bullets ripping through the metal skin of my Corsair.

Chance-Vought engineers had realized that the most vulnerable areas of the Corsair were the two oil coolers at the wing roots. The engineers reduced the danger posed by these "soft spots" by installing protective armor plate and two oil-cooler shut-off valves in the cockpit. With these valves a pilot could control the loss of oil from a damaged cooler. Unfortunately, during the years between WWII and Korea, someone in the Bureau of Aeronautics decided to remove the armor and disconnect the oil cooler shut-off controls. When those machine gun bullets tore through my airplane, they struck the oil cooler in the right wing root, and oil began to flow over the wing. I was dead meat from that point on.

These things don't come about as portrayed in the movies. There wasn't that burst of blackened castor oil from broken oil lines flowing back over Errol Flynn's goggles, no flicker of fire, no smoke pouring from under the instrument panel. Only some grinding noises as the engine began to suffer from the loss of its lifeblood, followed by a bunch of engine gauges starting to "peg," indicated that I was in deep trouble.

The cylinder head temperature, and the oil temperature needles hit the peg as the engine oil pressure dropped to zero. The next event was my attempt at keeping the corpse of my Pratt-Whitney radial engine running. As I turned toward the south I called Buck to tell him the obvious. Buck was already making a call to "Devastate Baker" to advise them of my plight.

I pulled the prop pitch to high to reduce the rpm and pushed the throttle to full power. Neither of these actions has support from aeronautical engineers, but I had heard this from Charles Lindbergh when he was teaching us how to conserve fuel when we were flying out of Emirau Island. The procedure worked for me once during WWII during a strike on Amami-O-Shima. That time, my Corsair had suffered a fatal hit, lost its oil, but continued to run for almost twenty minutes, long enough to carry me to more friendly waters before giving up.

This time I began a prayer that the engine would ignore all those less than desirable engine gauge readings, the red lined stuff, and would at least carry me back to a friendly locale as before. God always answers the prayers of stupid aviators. On this occasion, He answered mine with a resounding "No!" I suppose He felt that any dumbbell who knew better than to gun duel but still engaged in the sport deserved to have his stupidity punished.

A couple of minutes after being hit, I was down to nine hundred feet. I jettisoned the cockpit canopy, dropped my external fuel tank, pickled off my HVARS, and turned my dying machine toward an area that appeared to be a small tract of semi-flat cultivated land.

Actually, the area didn't offer many options because of the hilly terrain. I knew my Corsair with its dead engine could glide about thirteen miles from my beginning altitude to the flat spot that was about six or seven miles away.

All this was done as a reflex. I was lined up with the flat place on the ground when the engine gave its last gasp and died. My descent became steeper with the complete loss of power, and I tried to make sure I could fly the stricken machine to the place I had chosen for landing.

Buck slid into a position on my right wing and began to call out my altitude and airspeed. He started this litany by announcing that we were at two hundred feet altitude, flying at one hundred knots. Sometimes a pilot in distress will forget to consider these important points, attempt to stretch his glide, stall, and spin into the ground with guaranteed fatal results. Buck also told me that the most level plot of ground seemed to be a rather large rice paddy that was, by now, a couple of hundred yards ahead. I had already chosen that as the best spot to prang the bird, but I was thankful for a second opinion.

Photo courtesy of T. C. Crooson (AW)-323 "Death Rattlers"

I was about to overshoot the rice paddy, an event that would have me smashing into the earthen dike. Sudden stops at any speed can cause a lot of hurt. Hoping to assure a more gradual deceleration, I spiked the Corsair into the paddy water, an action that sent a less-than-fragrant spray splashing all over the place. My thought was that, if being drenched by the stench of human fertilizer was the worst thing to happen this day, I should be grateful. My dead Corsair stopped its forward movement within a hundred feet. I unsnapped the seat belt and shoulder harness and slid over the side into about two feet of the foulest smelling liquid that had ever assaulted my nose. There was a clump of thorny looking brush about thirty yards from where "old number 5" lay smoldering and hissing in the fetid water. I hobbled over and slithered under the brush to give myself some concealment while I counted my arms and legs and took a general stock of my situation.

Pilots spend a lot of spare time talking about airplanes and flying. This is sometimes referred to as "hangar flying." If you have doubts about the validity of this statement, ask any bartender at the officers club of any military air base. "Happy Hour" is a military ritual that began at military officers' clubs. They gathered at 1630 on Friday afternoons to celebrate the end of the workweek. It since has been adopted by civilian saloons and extended to every day of the week. Squadron pilots then, much like those of today, attended "Happy Hour" for drink, good fellowship, and "hangar-flying" sessions that often lasted for hours.

Among the subjects pilots often discussed in detail was the technique of "bailing out" of an airplane no longer able to stay in the air. Most pilots felt so secure in their aircraft that the mantra was, "Don't leave the plane, unless it is on fire or a wing is gone."

Another common subject was the technique of making crash landings (wheels up in water, gear down on dirt). Pilots picked the brains of those who had faced and had survived these situations. Lurking deep in every pilot's memory was a small, well-filled pocket of information just waiting for "that time."

It's a sort of reaction from back in the early days of flight training. In those times, our instructors often stressed the process of making a safe departure from a disabled aircraft. There was even a class taught in primary flight training where we practiced the proper procedures.

An old fuselage salvaged from a wrecked N2S had been mounted on high wooden trestles in the rear of the classroom building. Clad in full flight gear, including a parachute, and moving against a stopwatch, we had to climb an eight-foot ladder and slither over the side into a net. Monk Howie broke the air station record by three seconds, but he missed the net (not considered disqualifying) and broke his left arm. Treatment of his compound fracture required a two-week long sojourn in the base dispensary and the loss of training time while Monk practiced his vaunted swordsmanship with nurses who felt no need for romantic foreplay.

The navy seems to lose all perspective when faced with the thought of losing a promising aviator merely because he didn't know how, or when, to discard a crippled airplane. I always believed it was the loss of the investment to train a cadet rather than some emotional attachment to a cadet that motivated the navy's concerns.

When I suffered through the rigors of survival school back in '48, our instructors harped on the fact that once you are on the ground in enemy territory, your first move must be made with extreme caution. No move at all is sometimes the best, unless you are near your crashed airplane, which is a beacon marking your location for the enemy.

You hunker down and keep hidden as best you can and watch. Don't be too eager to begin that long walk home. Your first step may be toward unpleasant things.

Do take stock of what equipment you have that will be useful for your survival. Spend the first hours on the ground getting that gear packed for travel, and wait.

A glance at my watch told me that all my woes had occurred in less than fifteen minutes. Only a quarter of an hour had passed since I had that stroke of dumbness and broke my own rule against "gun dueling." I also figured that I was about ten, maybe fifteen or so miles from the place we had last spotted a small detachment of enemy troops.

My map of the area had suffered greatly from the soaking in the rice paddy. As I unfolded the paper, it disintegrated into a soggy, stinking mess. My best guess was that my crippled Corsair had carried me about twenty miles from the dueling site.

Buck and the lads had begun flying an orbit a few miles east of my crashed airplane. After I had been in my little cluster of brush for about twenty minutes, the three planes went into trail and began to dive toward something on the other side of some low hills five or so miles to the east of my crash site. Whatever they saw was posing a threat to my survival, and just before the Corsairs would disappear behind the hills I could see their HVAR rockets whooshing toward the targets I couldn't see. They climbed after the rocket attack and began a strafing run. The distance was such that the noise of their machine guns came to my position as a faint popping sound. As Jordan pulled out of his dive, something on the ground exploded with a great rumbling noise that was soon followed by a black, oily-looking cloud that rose above the hilltops somewhat like an Indian smoke signal of the Wild West. The flight circled their target area and must have decided that the threat had been removed.

From what I remembered, Buck would be able to stay and give me cover until about 0815. During the next three minutes, I hoped he would be able to make some contact with Search and Rescue, or maybe even lead a rescue helicopter to my position. But that helicopter thing was just so much wishful thinking. My position was at least seventy-five miles north of the 38th parallel, and even farther from the nearest friendly choppers, which didn't have much range anyhow.

Buck led his three Corsairs in a shallow dive almost over my spot in the brush, wagged his wings and headed back toward the ship. It was his flight now. The three had really pushed into their fuel reserves. I don't know why that fuel thing bothered me, considering my own problems, but it did. Maybe because I could still get a pretty good remembrance of a navy pilot who had a reputation for pushing his fuel reserves. One day his engine gasped its last just off the fantail, and he completed his tour in one of the ship's reefers zipped into a body bag.

Buck, Snick, and Jordan would be flying on fumes when they got back, but they would get back to the ship safely because they were good at what they did. I would spend the night camping in the woods because I had screwed up and done a stupid thing.

And that wing-wagging thing as they flew over me pissed me off. Dammit, I knew that was the only way they had for wishing me "good luck," but it made me resentful. I had done the same thing several times when my fuel gauge told me to go home after covering some poor downed soul, but this time it seemed so damned final.

Before the Corsairs were out of sight, four Douglas ADs lumbered into the Rescue CAP position. Buck, Snick, and Jordan must have done a good job on the Koreans because the AD Pilots just circled overhead and didn't make any attacks.

After the ADs had been overhead for an hour, I imagined that I could hear the "fluk-fluk-fluk" of chopper rotors. Most any noise can really carry a long way, especially in the canyons. Two of the ADs broke from their formation and flew south, out of sight.

The chopper, if there were one, could be from the Seoul area. I was straining my eyes toward the rotor noise when a sudden burst of some heavy automatic weapons fire spoiled my dream of rescue. The next sound was that of a chopper rotor running wild, then an explosion—and silence.

Those ADs continued their circling overhead. Obviously, no enemy troops were within their sight, so I decided it was time to move away from the crash site. It was impossible to keep hidden as I moved southeast toward some low hills that were covered by trees. The AD pilots stayed overhead, occasionally scouting ahead of my position for evidence of the enemy. I was having very good luck.

At about 1000 the four ADs were relieved from their RESCAP duties by four P-51 Mustangs that bore the "Whirling Meatball," the South Korean Air Force insignia.

A RESCAP stayed over my position as I moved toward the south. New flights would arrive to relieve others as they came to the end of their fuel. Each flight reached its minimum fuel level, about every hour and a half, until just after sunset.

By the time the last of my air protection deferred to darkness, I had moved almost five miles, and into some foothills. I crawled into a growth of thick brush and gave in to my fatigue. There would be no rescue this night.

Nightfall in the canyons comes rapidly. The last flight of my air cover was also navy ADs. They were still glinting in the waning sunlight when they flew over me and did that same damn wing-waggling salute thing, then turned west toward their carrier in the Yellow Sea. Now it really got lonely and darker. After that last flight left for home without my being relieved by another flight, I realized for the first time that I was neck deep in trouble. With that thought it seemed to get even lonelier and a whole lot darker.

I've had some lonely times. The first time I had been away from home for more than a week occurred when I entered the service back in 1942 and was sent off to flight school. During the first weeks, I enjoyed my freedom. I no longer had to share a bed with an older brother. I no longer had to submit to the whims of any one of my four sisters "because they are girls." And, except for the rigid rules of flight training, I could do as I pleased.

Then came the first rush of homesickness, and loneliness. However, these aches were short-lived. As time passed, they were eased out of my life by the increasing demands of military service. Eventually they were replaced by a need to have comrades nearby when I was trying to sleep. The sounds of battle, and the eerie scraping of land crabs scratching their way through South Pacific camps in their nocturnal search for food gave homesickness less importance. But even considering all my past loneliness, this quiet darkness alone in Korean woods was the acme of desolation. The last red glow of the setting sun was gone, and the area was as dark as I had ever seen. An overcast of thin clouds had rolled in to blank out even the faintest glow of stars. Blackness and quiet prevailed.

So far I hadn't seen any enemy troops or civilians, or even animals for that matter. Surely the North Koreans would be hunting me with vengeance in their hearts. God only knows how many of their countrymen we had killed back in the woods, but I was sure the casualty list was long enough to put some burning thoughts of revenge into their minds.

And Buck and the boys had surely slain a few more during the time they were flying cover for me. I determined that a move away from the area would be prudent.

Working under the theory that the "Snoop and Poop" Recon Troops knew what they were doing when they smeared black make-up on their faces, I spent the next twenty minutes rubbing dirt on the shining parts of my exposed anatomy. Next, I cut the harness webbing from my parachute canopy and stuffed some of the silk into my flight jacket. I had converted the jacket into a sort of knapsack by securing it around my waist with the zipper and using the sleeves to tie it around my neck. The parachute webbing would probably be a good item to keep. It had all those stout "D" rings and slide buckles, but I didn't have space in my "pack" to tuck it away. I scratched a shallow hole in the ground by a pine tree, buried the webbing, and covered the newly dug dirt with pine needles and leaves. In the darkness I couldn't see the results of my work, but the chances of some enemy dropping by and finding the stuff seemed pretty remote.

At 1940, after keeping a concentrated watch for movement for almost an hour, I decided to continue my trek toward the south. I thought it best to get as far from the site of my crashed Corsair as possible. Surely someone must have seen me crash, and the North Koreans were loath to let UN pilots get out of their land and back into the fight. For one thing, that spoils their propaganda. Parading a downed and downcast aviator before their civilian populace was thought to rouse them to the peak of patriotism.

Also, my position on the ground was well known to the folks on the carrier and God only knows who else. I had a strong belief that the UN Forces or the U.S. Marines would make another attempt to "extract" me come daylight. Their attempt would be made much easier if I could move to a flat, open area, away from the hills, a place that would be suitable for a chopper to land without being sniped by an enemy hidden in rough terrain. My mind kept wandering back to all those pre-Korean War experiments of ways to pick up downed pilots from the maw of the enemy. Even the experiments that worked required a large crew to set up the system of harnesses and cables, which seemed to me would mean a big sacrifice to save one man.

Buck, Snick, and Jordan would realize that I would move south as soon as feasible. We had discussed all these options often, and in depth. We spent a lot of time during our rare and clandestine drinking sessions talking about escape and evasion. Should any in the flight parachute out or crash land, the surviving members would be aware of the probable action of the downed member and know his intentions.

Night movement is difficult and hazardous even in the familiar confines of your bedroom. In an unfamiliar forest such movement causes much pain. There is no way I can recall how many times I tripped and fell on my face in the darkness. I do know that the last fall was one where I wondered if I had strength to get back on my feet.

By my inaccurate estimation, I had covered nearly five miles to the south when the eastern sky began to lighten, and I had to find a hiding place before full light. By 0530 I was again hunkered down in a small growth of woods, covered by dead tree limbs and pine needles. All around me was quiet, and the absence of North Koreans gave me confidence that I would soon be picked up and delivered back into the squadron fold. It didn't take long for weariness to take command. I slept, despite aching muscles and the rumble of an empty stomach.

For anyone attempting to escape from a wartime enemy, the possibility of getting shot increases in direct proportion to the irritability of the foe. Enemy soldiers, given their increased anger at having the added chore to their usual duties to search for and capture some escapee, are more inclined to lean toward the dead part of the "dead or alive" theory.

Chapter 9
Captured

The worst possible alarm clock comes in the form of an enemy boot prodding your ribcage. This one was persistent. It prodded my ribs, none too gently, until I came back to full consciousness. When my eyes and brain finally focused, I was staring into the muzzle of a 9mm automatic pistol held in the steady hand of a smiling NKPA captain. It is difficult for the uninitiated to imagine how large the hole in the muzzle of a 9mm pistol only inches from your eye looks in the dim light of a cloudy day.

Every action made toward a captured enemy of the armed forces of a totalitarian nation has the definite purpose of creating fear and a sense of despondency even before any interrogation begins. First, a captive is summarily relieved of all his belongings. This is designed to demonstrate complete dominance by the "People's" forces over their enemies.

The hoarded parachute silk, my squashed pack of cigarettes, flight jacket, gloves, watch, knife, pistol and holster, and survival kit were immediately taken from me. The captain examined each item, kept those he coveted, such as my pistol and Hamilton watch, and doled out the discards to his men. My captors were beginning to cast covetous eyes on my already tattered flight suit and my boondocker shoes, but I suppose they decided these items were of little value to any member of the search party. However, one of the soldiers continued to search through the many pockets of my orange flight suit and was rewarded with the discovery of my cigarette lighter, some lint and a few tobacco crumbs. He tried several times to ignite the lighter, but it was devoid of fluid.

Why pilots carry these leaky contraptions is a mystery to me. Usually, when the lighter fluid seeps out at altitude, it causes painful burns in the vicinity of the pocket. When called into action, a lighter filled with fluid will very often flare up to the point of igniting the user's hand and singeing his eyebrows. Once, my gentlemanly instincts led me to lighting a lady's cigarette with a fully charged lighter and destroyed what could have become a beautiful relationship.

After looting my possessions, they tied my hands behind my back, and placed me under the watchful eye of a young soldier who kept his rifle pointed at my head. The assigned guard watched my every move. It was obvious that, if left to his own devices, he would rather shoot me than spend his time watching over me. He would move away and seem to relax his vigilance, glancing to the thick brush thicket that was only yards away. This guy wanted me to attempt an escape, which would allow him to fire a bullet into my head, thereby relieving him of his onerous duty.

Suddenly the captain snarled an order that made everyone of the patrol hit the dirt. I could hear the unmistakable growl of R-2800 engines coming into the area low and fast. The captain crawled over to me and placed the muzzle of what, moments ago, had been my Smith and Wesson 38 cal. pistol, close to my left ear. From his actions I could assume that if I made any attempt to signal the Corsairs, it would be my last act on this earth.

The four Corsairs passed directly over our little bivouac in the stand of trees and continued north. The engine noises and a rising hope that I would soon be saved faded as the planes continued on their mission. I remembered the plight of the air force pilot who was the object of our very cursory search yesterday on our way to incinerate that truck convoy.

As soon as the planes could no longer be heard, two NKPA privates, acting none too gently, removed the bonds from my wrists and replaced them with a new set of ties. My ankles and wrists were tied together behind my back, much as a hog is trussed for a trip to the slaughterhouse. My hands and feet began tingling as my blood circulation and nerves fell victim to the tight ropes. I tried to loosen the ropes by expanding my muscles and the effort brought on a painful "charley horse" in my right leg.

Next a dirty cloth that had a faint odor of kerosene was tied over my eyes as a blindfold, and secured very tight with a huge lumpy knot over the bridge of my nose. I wondered how these little men could find the muscle power to tie things so tightly. Four men picked me up and carried me some distance through the woods where I was tossed into the bed of a truck that smelled of blood and puke.

The truck was driven out of the woods back onto the road. At this point in my career as a POW, I was hoping the Corsairs wouldn't return. When they saw an enemy truck speeding down a Korean country lane they just naturally dove down and popped it with a rocket.

So far as I could determine, we traveled for perhaps twenty miles. During the drive, I tried to decipher sounds and the causes of the many bumps, twists and turns the truck made. Maybe the recollection of this would be of help if I could escape again.

The truck bumped over a set of railroad tracks, splashed through a shallow stream, and finally stopped in a small grove of trees. My captors dragged me from the bed of the vehicle and carried me to a sort of stockade constructed of timber and concertina wire. Inside the stockade, an NKPA soldier who reeked of garlic and body filth removed my bonds and blindfold. There were four other prisoners in the stockade, three very young, extremely terrified American soldiers wearing the shoulder patch of the First Cavalry Division. The fourth American, I presumed, was that F-80 pilot we had looked for yesterday. He was sitting tied to a tree fifty feet back in the woods. Someone had made a splint from a tree branch and had strapped it to his left leg. I nodded to him, but he made no response.

The demeanor of the three soldiers was enough to convince me they would be of no help in any escape attempt. These youngsters avoided eye contact, and when I looked toward them, each man would turn away and stare at the ground. I got the feeling, from the sly glances they made when they thought I wasn't looking, that because I was an officer, they believed that I should "do something." After all, they had been told officers were supposed to care for their men.

These soldiers had already been completely cowed by the North Koreans. Since the beginning of the Korean fighting, we had heard many tales of young United States' soldiers who had been enticed into the post-WWII army with the promise that they would be sent on occupation duty in the country of their choice. These unfortunates were given a few weeks of rudimentary basic training, and then shipped out. When they arrived in their chosen Duty Country, they came filled with the anticipation of spending the four years of their enlistment at easy duty. There would be wine and hundreds of wild sex-starved native women to ease their burdens. Advancing their military knowledge was furthest from their minds. They were supposed to be given training within their assigned units, an advanced combat schooling designed to increase their military skills and physical prowess, training they had never received. Instead, after spending their time in the Oriental Sodom, they had suddenly found themselves in a shooting war with no idea of what they should do or how to do it.

These unfortunates often selected surrender to the enemy as a means of escaping the horrors of battle and saving their lives. Most of them had been taught the idealism of the section of the Geneva Convention regarding treatment of POWs. They would shortly face a rude awakening that Asian soldiers believe that those who surrendered should receive nothing in the form of food and medical treatment.

A sentry growled something and prodded me with his bayonet, words and actions that I took to mean I was neither to move near to nor to speak to the soldiers.

A few minutes later, he untied my hands and escorted me from the stockade to a nearby tent. A folding cot, two chairs and a small table occupied the tent. I was seated in one of the chairs and offered food in the form of some garlicky cabbage mixture laced with peppers, and an American canteen cup of water that smelled of chlorine and pond slime.

At this point in my experience as a downed pilot and POW, I had had neither food nor water. I resisted the temptation to vomit, failed in my determination to refuse the food and drink, and ate and drank of the offering.

This meal was my introduction to kimchi, the spicy national dish of Korea. It didn't taste as rank as it smelled, but the hot peppers were intimidating, even for one who had been raised on Tex-Mex food and jalapeno peppers. The food was very filling for a stomach that had been blessed with only that small carton of corn flakes about thirty-six hours ago. The kimchi eliminated the angry, empty growl of my insides almost immediately, but soon replaced that with a snarling, cramping rumble of a bowel bulging with gas generated by that heavily spiced cabbage.

Chapter 10
Interrogation

Communism has trained its military interrogators to employ infinite and finely tuned methods for extracting desired information from their enemies. Their methods were honed to perfection in the torture dungeons of the old OGPU, which was the Soviet secret police from 1922 to 1935, and were developed during thousands of interrogations of citizens of the USSR who had been deemed enemies of the Soviet Union. In the early days of the revolution, the state interrogators relied on brute strength to exact the exquisite pain that resulted in a spate of information. As time passed, methods of torture were refined and developed to a science that was subtler but gained the same result.

The main shortcoming of this system is that it is vulnerable to resistance. Citizens in the hands of the Soviet police who realized that the game was up became tactile and responded to questions even before their fingernails were completely pulled.

But most United States military men resisted strongly. They gained their strength to resist from a life of personal freedom. Their obstinacy often rendered the Soviet-trained intelligence agents impotent.

Anyone who has completed any escape and survival course has been schooled in the basics of Communistic interrogation. People thus schooled will recognize Communist techniques and be forearmed by that knowledge.

Interrogators usually begin a session by exuding charm, friendship, and solicitude, showing their captive a deep concern for his plight along with their often-stated willingness to inform the International Red Cross as to the state of his well being. During the initial contact, a soldier who is senior in rank to the captive represents the enemy. He is always well-groomed and dressed in a clean, well pressed, and finely-tailored uniform while his prisoner is still wearing the clothing in which he was captured.

The prisoner is usually tired, hungry, dirty, sometimes bleeding, and always apprehensive about his future. In contrast to his captor, he is presenting a poor expression of military bearing and appearance.

The interrogator begins his routine with casual conversation interspersed with occasional non-questions. During this period he exhibits his heartfelt feeling of friendship for his brothers-in-arms and his desire to aid this unfortunate in his present predicament.

But once his conversation turns toward his real objective, which is to gain military information, there is a subtle change in his tone of voice. And his eyes become steely, as does his demeanor.

I had finished my meal when an NKPA major blustered into the tent and sat down. He wore an impeccable uniform. His boots were polished to a mirror shine, the creases in his trousers were razor sharp, and he obviously had come directly from a shower and a shave. He absolutely reeked of some mysterious Oriental scent that almost, but not quite, blended with the keen smell of the kimchi that hung in the tent.

Of course, my clothing was in blatant contrast, being a dirty and sweaty flight suit, salt-stained and spotted with a variety of airplane oil, hydraulic fluid, remnants of that last, hurried cup of coffee, and other sundry liquids. The major's face shone with the gloss of his recent shave, and his hair was combed with a part that was arrow straight. My last shave was now almost two days old, and I stank with the residue of the rice paddy and the sweat of both the fear of the unknown and physical exertion.

The major offered me a Camel cigarette and a small khaki colored book of "gopher" matches, both of which had been taken from a package of captured K rations "liberated" by the NKPA during their initial successes. He obviously meant this tactic to demonstrate the superiority of the NKPA over the UN Forces. While I was his prisoner, reduced to virtual slavery, he was living the good life on captured American luxuries.

As I smoked the cigarette, the NKPA officer opened an American C ration can of wieners and beans with an American can opener and scooped a mouthful with the spoon from an American mess kit. The major favored me with a gleaming, toothy smile, and introduced himself as an officer of the NKPA Intelligence while he chewed the food with obvious relish.

When the major took his seat, it became obvious that his chair was taller than mine. This was another subtle piece of the interrogation program planned so that I would be looking up at him. He offered me another small pack of cigarettes and a book of matches, again items taken from K ration packs. This was designed to show that the kindly NKPA was allowing me to have the leftovers from their conquests.

I was being shown that the NKPA was the ruling entity on this peninsula, and that they were making full use of captured military items abandoned by the Americans as they ran in fear from the initial NKPA attack. Invincibility of the Communists was the theme being subtly impressed on me.

In his almost accent-free English he began to engage me in officer-to-officer social chitchat that was meant to put me at ease. He asked me if I had attended his Alma Mater, UCLA. Was Hollywood still a good place to enjoy the favors of beautiful starlets? And did the Cirque Room at Long Beach still serve those delicious meals? We were equals. We could easily become friends.

But when the major asked for information about the deployment of UN forces, his eyes took on an iron glint that promised painful treatment should that information not be forthcoming. Behind the forced smile and the stern façade, there lurked promises of some severe and painful Chinese torture.

When I answered his queries with my name, rank, and serial number for the third time, the benevolent major reached across the table and struck me in the face with a blow that sent me reeling from my chair. The just lit cigarette flew across the tent and out through the open tent flap. A soldier picked it up and took a long deep puff. Nice time and friendship between brothers-at-arms had come to a painful and abrupt end.

Chapter 11
Liberated

The sun was getting low, a fact that the Koreans couldn't hide. Suddenly two soldiers entered the tent, yanked me to my feet, half dragged me to a nearby pick-up-like truck, and tossed me into its bed. I couldn't see clearly, and the truck was started with some difficulty and much chatter between the Koreans. We began to bounce down what passed as a road. I knew that my interrogator's grilling was just the warm-up for more intensive and sophisticated questioning elsewhere. But where?

We had gone perhaps fifteen miles toward the setting sun when I suddenly heard the unmistakable sounds of Corsair engines. The truck driver increased the speed of his vehicle, careening down the narrow lane while searching desperately for a place to hide but to no avail.

I had often wondered what it was like on the ground during an attack by a flight of Corsairs. Before they roared into the area, the quiet of the countryside had been disturbed only by the noise of the truck engine. The Koreans had been chatting and calmly smoking cigarettes as if they had few cares in the world. Then, like a magical illusion, the Corsairs were upon us. I hoped they would decide not to waste a napalm tank on a single truck.

As if to continue my education of war on the ground, a violent explosion only a few yards forward shattered the windshield and sent shards of metal and glass through the driver and his passenger. The gray fabric that covered the truck bed was suddenly a tatter of rags. Bomb fragments punctured the sides of the truck, and my ears rang with the pain of concussion.

With a dead man at the wheel, the truck swerved off the road, bounced over the shallow ditch, and crashed into a deep brush-filled ravine. As the rocket-blasted truck bounced along on its wild ride into the ravine, I was violently tossed about, bouncing from one side of the truck bed to the other. My body was smashed into every unyielding brace and fillet a truck bed could have. Twice I felt stabs of pain as my body encountered the jagged metal where bomb fragments had torn through the bed of the truck. Blood from the bodies of my late escorts poured into the cargo compartment and flowed into the lowest corner of the bed.

It seemed an eternity before the truck finally crashed to an abrupt stop in a clump of thick brush. My inertia catapulted me through the remains of the thin canvas truck-bed canopy. I flew through the air with the ease and grace of a trussed-up hog, caromed off a shattered tree branch, and ended my flight in a small brushy clump of some garlicky-smelling plant, the national odor of Korea.

I took time to evaluate the state of my battered body. After deciding some body movement could be accomplished, I began to disentangle myself from the brush. This proved to be a difficult task. My hands and feet were still bound, and my legs had managed to loop themselves over a stout branch. Release from the embrace of brush took nearly a half-hour of strenuous labor, after which I fell about six feet to the ground. By the time I managed to get on my feet the Corsairs were gone, and the truck was beginning to burn. The two wheels not embedded in the dirt were still turning slowly. Smoke poured from under the hood, and the smell of gasoline boded imminent explosion.

Both the driver and his companion were still sitting in their seats, obviously quite dead. The fragments of whatever it was the Corsair pilot had used to destroy the truck had ripped the hood from the engine, demolished the front of the cab, and torn the flesh from the faces of the truck crew.

I found a jagged shard of metal torn from what had been one of the truck's fenders. I slipped my bonds over the jagged metal and used the sharp edge to saw through the ropes that bound my wrists. That I managed this feat without inflicting serious wounds on my wrists gave me confidence. With my hands free, it was easy to untie my ankles.

Once freed, I began to evaluate the state of my health and well-being. Blood seeped from my nose and from a deep cut over my left eye. My right shoulder drooped. My right leg reluctantly held up my weight, and I quickly lost count of the assaulting aches and pains.

The attack on the truck seemed to have gone unnoticed by any North Korean forces. As the truck hissed from leaking, steaming liquids, I took a rifle and a bandoleer of ammunition from one of the bodies and a knife from the other. There was a full canteen of water on the cab floor, and a rolled U. S. Army blanket tucked behind the seat. I found no food, but felt suitably equipped to start a long walk south.

The ravine, the final resting place of the truck and its two soldiers sloped downhill to become the bed of a small stream. In the growing darkness, it seemed to be flowing south, and I wanted to go south as fast as prudently possible.

Chapter 12
On the Run

I followed the winding stream about two hundred yards when the undergrowth became too thick to penetrate. I moved to my left about a hundred yards and climbed to the top of a small hill. From a new vantage point, I could see the road we had traveled and the now blazing remains of the scene of my escape. As I watched, a five-man enemy foot-patrol appeared around a bend in the road a quarter mile away and soon found the wreckage.

They could see that enemy aircraft had destroyed the truck and its two occupants. Since the past August, this was a common fate for North Korean vehicles and their drivers, but the patrol couldn't have known that a POW had escaped after the wreck. At any rate, the members of the patrol seemed more interested in dinner than in looking for me. After they had pulled their dead comrades from the wreck and covered the bloody corpses with a blanket, one of the Koreans began to build a small cook fire. While they were occupied with preparing dinner, I left the area.

Walking through woods at night isn't an easy task under the best of conditions. I was proceeding along at a rapid pace through unfamiliar woods on the property of unfriendly people, all the while attempting to remain under cover

As my march through the gathering darkness progressed, low tree branches lashed my face while erosion-bared tree roots caused me to trip and fall, causing new pain and bleeding. The countless falls made it harder to overcome the urge to lie down and rest.

But with the memory of that NKPA major, came the urge to rise and overcome the pain of injuries and sore muscles. The rifle and ammunition became a problem as I moved through the night. The rifle seemed determined to entangle on every low-hanging tree limb, and the bandoleer of ammunition gained weight with each footstep. I began to compare the benefit of the weapon in assisting my evasion of the enemy against the expenditure of my strength, which the rifle required.

If I were to meet just one North Korean, the rifle could save my ass. But if I were to be confronted by as few as two of the enemy, and tried to defend myself with that unfamiliar rifle, it would serve only to get me killed. I scraped out a shallow hole in the rough earth and put the rifle and bandoleer of ammunition to rest. I trudged on against building fatigue.

As light began to color the eastern skies, I tripped over a sharp stone outcropping and fell again. Inertia caused me to tumble down the hillside for about ten yards. The fall re-opened the cut on my head, and I came to a stop on a flat slab of stone projecting from the hillside. Erosion from rain had formed a shallow cave about six feet deep and two feet high.

Tree roots and brush pretty well hid this small grotto, which looked to be an excellent place for a good day's sleep. I crawled inside, rolled myself in the captured blanket, and soon drifted into the sleep of the innocent, despite my pains. Just before I dropped off, I counted the places in my body that ached. Two or three bruises I hadn't noticed before, which had occurred during my crash in the rice paddy, began to assert themselves.

When I awoke it must have been about 1800. Since the Koreans had liberated my watch, I estimated the time by using the position of the sun. This wasn't my greatest talent. Despite the many times I had spent trying to get back aboard the *Badoeng Strait* before dark, I had never seen a need to relate the position of the sun with the position of the hands of my watch. When I felt the need to know the time, I found myself automatically glancing at my watchless wrist. The sun was low on the horizon and was just minutes from dropping behind a bank of clouds. I recalled that after 1900 all landings aboard the ship were entered into the logbooks as night landings, so I guessed that it was sometime between 1800 and 1900. That was close enough for my work.

My mind was now becoming cluttered with thoughts about my needs. I had used most of the water in the canteen, some to drink, some to cool the soreness of my many hurts. My bloody nose had streaks of crusted blood, thick gobs of the stuff that made breathing difficult. When I tried to remove those red snots, the bleeding started again. After many attempts, I was able to soak them away. My breathing was easier then, but I decided my nose had been broken, either during the plane crash, the "love tap" that NKPA major had given me, or by my involvement in the truck wreck. I knew only that I could see my nose without crossing my eyes.

I needed food. One of the bothersome aches was in my empty stomach. This section of Korea wasn't a place that afforded much possibility of living off the land. But I had distilled my needs down to two vital requirements. First and foremost was the overwhelming need to concentrate on escaping and evading all human beings. Without this as my goal, the physical things, such as the need for food and drink would be moot. The second need was, of course, food and water, both necessary to retain the physical strength to continue my march to the south.

The covering shadows of the dark Korean night signified it was time to begin moving. I tried to remember the current phase of the moon. I didn't remember if there had been any moonlight last night, and I didn't recall even thinking about the moon before I put myself into my present circumstance. No matter, it was almost time to move out.

I began what had become my pre-sunset ritual of staring about the countryside looking for movement and listening for sounds that would foretell human presence—and hoping no one was in sight. I was amazed at what seemed to be the abandonment of this part of North Korea by its civilians.

Communist countries have a habit of sterilizing a strip of the land inside their border with a democratic nation. In their paranoid attempt to keep their citizens at home, and the capitalist citizens out, they completely clear the border strip of places that may afford cover and concealment from the omnipresent border guards. But my rather faulty estimation told me that I was still at least fifty miles north of the 38th parallel. Any sterilized border areas with their barbed wire concertinas and land mines are usually only a few miles wide.

In the gathering gloom, I could see two ox carts accompanied by five Korean civilians trundling along a road. As soon as deeper darkness covered the countryside, I moved out.

I had no idea of the exact time I had collapsed early yesterday morning and had fallen asleep in my cave. As daylight approached this morning, I began searching for a place to hole up during the daylight hours. I fought fatigue and muscle soreness that screamed at me just to lie down and think, "to hell with it all." That fall the day before and the tumble down the hillside to the entrance of that small grotto was the best thing that had happened to me so far.

It had led to a warm, dry, and secure place to spend the day and certainly reduced my body fatigue. Today the best place I could find was a small tod on top of a low hill. Noises I couldn't decipher awakened me intermittently during the day, making me instantly cognizant of the soreness that had encompassed my entire body.

According to the position of the sun, it was some time after noon when what sounded like the bawl of a cow drifted up the hillside. My muscles rebelled even more as I moved out of the small clump of brush to look around. Stabbing fires of pain, defined each of my movements. A small herd of goats, driven along the path by a young Korean girl, created the noise. She was clad in a long skirt and one of those short blouses that left her midriff bare. Whenever one of her charges would balk, she would lash at it with a stick. And when the goatherd shouted at an animal, the beast bleated back at the girl. Their direction would bring them close to my hiding place. I began to consider the unpleasant possibility of having to kill a young girl.

To make matters worse the weather had become much cooler since I had gone to sleep. Although the sun was shining, the sky had taken on a grayish cast. The sun wore a wide halo among some mare's-tail clouds, and the wind was freshening from the north. We had always been told that the Korean Peninsula ignored the fall season, and made a sudden leap from the heat and dust of summer into the cold and dust of winter. When I had fallen into my stupor early this morning, I was covered with sweat generated by the combining triad of fear, exertion, and doubt.

This afternoon, when the animal noises woke me, I was chilled and shaking, and each shake only intensified the pain. And I was hungry. My total intake of food since 0300 yesterday hadn't been enough to offer subsistence to a small boy. My mind couldn't seem to think of anything but one of those combat ration chocolate bars, the ones that were created back during WWII so as not to melt in tropical climes. They resembled a square chunk of brownish flint stone in taste and consistency back in 1944. They had not improved with age. During WWII the tropical climate was unable to melt the bars, but the heat made them chewable to a degree. I had tried to eat one of the chocolate hunks back aboard ship, but the cooler indoor climate and the age of the chocolate had cured them into a brick-like substance. But in my present circumstance I would have relished the texture and taste of just one of those bars.

My thoughts of food were quickly dismissed when the sound of human voices drifted in on the gusty wind. I chanced another look from my brush clump. At the foot of the hill, four small trees grew beside a narrow footpath. Under those trees, sitting in the shade with their backs to the wind, two elderly Koreans had taken up residence on a flat stone to the left of the footpath.

Both men wore the stiffly lacquered black hats that marked the esteemed "Papa-San," and were smoking cigarettes in those small Korean pipes. The aroma wafted up the hillside and reminded me of my favorite Camel cigarettes.

One of the men finished his smoke and removed a small flat tin and chopsticks from a bindle he had placed on the ground. He opened the tin and ate some of what looked like rice. I thanked the Great God that I couldn't smell the food. Even the lure of the cigarette smoke was almost more than my senses could bear.

After the North Koreans had finished their meal, they enjoyed another cigarette. Then they packed their belongings and continued on their way. I wondered if perhaps there could be a village nearby. I decided "what if there is," then fell asleep again. This time I had the sense to wrap myself in the blanket I had stolen from the bombed truck. When I next awoke, it was dark, very quiet, and much, much colder. I estimated the time to be about 1900. The only thing that gave me an idea of the time of day was that low streak of reddish glow lingering in the western sky.

In these days, the "weather guessers" opened and closed their meteorological days with times they referred to as BOMT and EOET. BOMT denoted the "beginning of morning twilight," an official start of the new daylight. And EOET was the "end of evening twilight," and stated that darkness was covering our part of the earth.

I also recalled that only last week my flight was kept "on station" just south of Oijongbu while we were supporting a battalion of "Chesty" Puller's regiment. The battalion was in the van of the marine division, and was having a tough go against an enemy that was laying down heavy mortar fire from the reverse slope of a hill. Artillery fire couldn't do much against such enemy emplacements, so they called in air support. We could hit the enemy from their rear, and had finally jarred them loose from their positions.

"Chesty" could have done the job without air support, but at a greater cost to his regiment, and "Chesty" really hated to lose marines if he didn't have to. So we stayed around popping small units until we were out of ordnance and low on fuel. We finally got back to the *Badoeng Strait* about 1900. That was the first time since 1948 that I was faced with the challenge of making a night landing.

All of us had decided long ago that our landing signal officer was blind even in the daylight. At night he would probably give us a "cut" far enough from the flight deck to give us a perfect landing, but into the fantail of the ship, an area referred to as the "spud locker."

When we returned from the Puller mission, there had been only that little pink gleam of light on the western horizon, which was about what I was seeing now. Since we landed at 1915, I estimated the time to be about the same.

So after my usual "watch and listen" time, I began my nightly trek. For the first couple of hours, I just couldn't seem to get my tired limbs to work properly. Walking down a small hill wasn't bad, but then as luck would have it, there was always an "uphill" to follow every "downhill." Yet I wanted to continue on what I hoped was my route home. The next hill seemed more like one of the Alps. I had begun to believe the damn thing was akin to the Matterhorn, and when I finally reached the crest, I was exhausted.

Far to the south at the extreme limits of visibility, I could see the dim starlight reflecting from what looked like the junction of two rivers. My fading memory of the maps of the area marked that point as the juncture of the Imjin River and a tributary stream just a few miles northeast of the town of Inch'on.

Inch'on was on the highway between Sariwon and Kumhwa. This was the same place we had attacked and incinerated those trucks in the early morning of the 15th. That incident was only three days ago, but it seemed like a year. If I could find the place that we had bombed, I would really have a way to get myself oriented for the rest of my long walk home.

As I recalled, the trucks had pulled off the road about halfway between the Imjin and the Yesong Rivers. If I could get there, I would be only thirty or so miles north of the 38th Parallel. My attempts at calculating my position were tainted by my desire to "think" myself closer to American troops than I really was.

If the marines were having any luck, they would now have recaptured Seoul, and the North Koreans would be back across the 38th Parallel. If there was any good luck in this dreadful situation, the damn war would be over, and I would soon be eating American food and sipping a Jack Daniels sour mash.

Just as the eastern sky was brightening, I holed up on the north side of the Sariwon road. Before I went to sleep, I found a stick and drew a map in the dirt of what I could remember of the area. I decided that if my map had any degree of accuracy, the truck that had been taking me to prison camp had gone about thirty miles before it came to grief in that ravine. A larger tributary flowed into the creek where the bombed truck had crashed, so my first recognizable landmark must have been the Nan River.

All this was interesting, but didn't serve to satisfy my hunger. By now my captured canteen was almost empty, creating yet another problem that vainly cried for a solution. The first rays of dawn's light tipped some of the high clouds when I found what seemed a good place for a day's snooze. During my two days of foot travel through the mysterious Orient, I had discovered that the Korean people rarely walked over the hills. Thus, by confining my travels to the ridge tops as much as possible and avoiding the flat, cultivated lands, I would have the best chance of avoiding any unfriendly folks carrying rifles.

One very important and basic rule of escape and evasion is, "DO NOT GIVE IN TO THE URGE TO TAKE A DAY OFF." Even though movement through enemy territory has its dangers, the act of sitting in one place waiting for others to save you presents a peril that outweighs those of continual movement. If you should decide to establish a camp, even if that base is well hidden in some remote area, it will tend to lull you into reducing your vigilance.

The first thing you know you will have decided that no one is around to see or smell the smoke, and the next thing you know, you have build yourself a fire to warm your bones. Ultimately, you begin scrounging within your self-proclaimed territory for food, and these two actions are enough to get you caught. It's like hanging a sign that says, "Here I am," as you leave traces of your presence about your "permanent camp site" that will soon get you either dead or have you serving a tour in some prison camp in Mongolia.

Hunger created a constantly growing stab of pain in my belly. The people who should know say that after a few days without a meal the stomach "converts," and the feeling of hunger goes away or at least diminishes, as the body begins to consume its excess fat. This was the third day of my travels since my last meal. My stomach still hurt, and I hadn't noticed any so-called "gastric conversion."

As I began my evening stroll through the exotic Orient, I heard clearly the clatter of a radial engine. The aircraft had to be one of the night fighters of VMF (N) 513 because for all I knew, there were no other pilots who flew around in the darkness looking for things to blow up. The plane passed overhead heading north. A short time later other engine noises destroyed the night calm. This latest racket was accompanied by the clash of shifting truck gears and the whine of overworked, overloaded and under-maintained vehicles moving in convoy.

According to my calculations, I was only a couple miles from one of the few major roads in this area. Crossing a well-traveled highway would pose a serious problem. It would require traversing a rather wide, cleared area in addition to the road itself. This would keep me away from any means of concealment for an extended period of time. Even in the darkness, my being in an open area would increase the possibility of capture.

Cultivated fields, cleared of trees and brush, bordered the main roads and offered very little concealment for a fugitive crossing the open grain fields and rice paddies.

From what I remembered after flying missions over this country, these open spaces could be several hundred yards wide. A quarter of a mile of walking, day or night, out in plain view of God and everyone else was a prospect that scared the hell out of me.

I considered moving parallel to the open space hoping to find an area where the road moved through a forest or over a stream. But even if I could find such an area, the extra miles might be more than my weakening state could tolerate. I discarded the idea.

If I got lucky and survived that perilous road crossing, I would need some time afterward to find a place to hide during the approaching daylight. I decided to cross the open areas just before the beginning of morning twilight, and then to use whatever darkness remained to find a hiding place for the new day. It was a lot to accomplish before dawn.

And in my few days of evasion experience, that early dawn seemed to be the time when farmers awoke to begin their chores, and NKPA soldiers started their military actions.

Chapter 13
Carnage

My approximate speed of movement had been about one mile per hour. For the past two nights, well before the early morning light, I had begun to look for a place to spend the day. It would be prudent to stop an hour early, sacrifice a mile or so of progress, and reduce the risk of being caught at daybreak when Korean farmers began moving about the land.

I scratched out a shallow hole in the earth atop a low hill and gathered some loose brush with which to cover myself for the day. Unexpectedly, I heard a Corsair engine as the pilot went into an orbit. It seemed to be circling over that same road that I had decided not to cross.

Suddenly the brilliance of a magnesium flare ruptured the darkness. The Corsair entered a dive toward the lead truck in the noisy convoy moving down the road. Bombs and rockets burst, machine guns chattered, and blasts of exploding trucks filled the night. Peering through the brush covering, I could see the looming ground fires reddening the darkness over the road I had to cross tomorrow evening.

Then I caught the sound of another aircraft engine approaching south of my position. When that second plane arrived, the first night fighter flew low over the convoy for a last look at the carnage he had wrought, and then departed the area heading south. The second Corsair, also from VMF (N) 513, guided by the flames, began to attack any undamaged vehicles. There were twenty trucks on the road with no place to hide.

The second Corsair pilot had no need to pop another flare. He continued the destruction for another fifteen minutes. Then, with his ordnance exhausted, he turned south and melted into the darkness. Dawn glowed almost as red as the fire from the wreckage. There was no movement down on the road or anywhere else as far as I could see. The North Koreans had a real talent for keeping out of harm's way.

My stomach began to dominate my good sense and training. Although my brain was occupied mainly with the thought of escape, my stomach cried out for something to eat. I was at my usual level of fatigue. However, my soreness had diminished to a level that allowed me to relax. Considering the distraction caused by the convoy, I believed that my hiding place would be as secure as possible.

But somehow the day just wasn't meant to be one that would allow me to rest. A plethora of noises kept me awake, and my stomach constantly reminded me that I needed food. And I really didn't have the slightest idea of how I would find some.

September 20 dawned cool and sunny, with fluffy little clouds drifting toward the north. A slight breeze blew in from the south carrying the faint sounds of oxen bellowing as they pulled their plows. Men shouted at the protesting oxen, and women talked as they did their chores. As much, or as little, as I dared to reveal my position, I crawled to the edge of the hill to survey the area. A squad of the NKPA soldiers was working in the carnage left by the night fighters, pulling charred bodies from the wrecks and loading the corpses onto three ox carts.

About twenty minutes passed when two P-51s abruptly appeared flying low and fast. The suddenness of their arrival caused the work party to drop the dead soldiers and dive for cover. The Mustangs flew over the burning trucks looking for something to shoot. After two passes up the line of wrecks, they decided there was nothing to be blown up, and turned south for their long flight home.

At morning's first light, a flight of four Corsairs bearing the logo of VMF 214, Pappy Boyington's Black Sheep Squadron, suddenly appeared low and fast from the west, scattering the mortuary crew into the trees. These pilots flew over the wreckage and also decided there was nothing left of the convoy that was worth the expenditure of ordnance. Fighter pilots like to blow things up. They experience no greater thrill than to watch that initial explosion of a target, but they are loath to waste their bombs, rockets, bullets, and napalm on smoldering wreckage.

A lot of the rural Korean roads were nothing more than narrow strips of packed earth, about ten feet wide, separating the flooded rice paddies. The raised areas were built up using soil excavated from the rice paddies. Over the years, farmers used the path to move their ox carts among the flooded fields during the planting, cultivating, and harvesting of crops. This constant use of makeshift roads packed the surface hard enough to support the travel of military supply vehicles off the major highways, which had become extremely hazardous since the prior June.

Because they were narrow and mostly bordered by water, they denied a truck driver space to maneuver his vehicle. That characteristic also allowed a single night-fighter pilot to destroy a large convoy of trucks once he spotted them in the darkness.

Sighting a moving convoy in the darkness wasn't always difficult. NKPA "convoy discipline" wasn't very good. The drivers had a fatal habit. They often wanted to see where they were going and would use their headlights, flashing them on and off as they drove down the narrow paths. A night-fighter pilot flying at ten thousand feet could see in an instant the flashing light from miles away. One second of light was often enough.

Once that instant flash of light was spotted, a magnesium parachute flare was dropped to illuminate the sky over the expected target. The fighter pilot would dive under his self-made sunshine and disable the lead truck of the convoy, effectively blocking the narrow road and bringing all vehicles of the convoy to a dead stop. Next, the pilot attacked the last truck in the convoy reducing it to a heap of smoldering rubble and putting a cork into the bottle. The trucks were unable to turn around and run because the roadway was too narrow. Thus, the whole core of the line of trucks was trapped, allowing the fighter to continue his mission to the limit of his fuel and ordnance.

Some of the drivers, in their desperate attempt to escape the carnage, tried to turn their vehicles, but they only managed to slide off the hard surface into the soft, stinking mud of the paddies. Other members of the truck crews leaped from their vehicles and ran back down the road or braved the stench of the paddy water, which they preferred to being strafed.

There was still enough darkness at ground level to give me concealment, so I continued to move, hoping I wouldn't run into any of the Korean truck drivers and hoping to salvage something from the trucks.

Just before sunrise, some P-51 Mustangs of the South Korean Air Force made strafing runs down the row of burned out trucks. They restarted several small fires, but the flight of Corsairs had done their job well, and the new fires burned out quickly for want of combustibles.

Truck convoys are used to carry supplies to the front line troops, and I fondly hoped to find some food and water to. The idea of food, even food partially incinerated, drove me to chance movement during the tailings of the night.

Wading waist-deep across a flooded, well-fertilized rice paddy is the worst experience a Westerner could encounter in his life. Perhaps the mortal sinner who has a weak stomach and a sensitive nose will escape from the fires of Hell only to be condemned to stand neck deep in the Hades version of a Korean rice paddy. But the fetid water of a rice paddy also affords good concealment. After our planes have attacked a specific place and wrought their destruction, the NKPA seems to avoid the area until they are sure they will not be greeted by a repeat performance.

Chapter 14
Scavenging

I managed to cover the distance to the road during morning twilight. Dead North Koreans littered the landscape. Most of them had leaped from their trucks and were killed as they tried to run. There were moans coming from some of the wounded soldiers, sounds that were difficult for my Christian ethos to ignore. But aided by some small fires that still flickered among the trucks, I was able to glean some needed supplies, including some food.

The salvageable food was mostly cooked rice packed into small, quart-sized, metal containers. Many of these had been destroyed, but I found two intact cans that had been blown from the trucks. A number of small flat tins containing some sort of fish product and some flimsy wooden boxes of round flat loaves of hard bread also had scattered among the wreckage.

One of the trucks in the center of the convoy was riddled with fifty caliber bullet holes but had not burned. This truck had been carrying a cargo of beer that the bullets had converted into a foamy mass of broken brown glass. In my rapid search I found only two bottles that had somehow survived the attack.

I gathered my loot, stowed it as best I could in a pack made from NKPA uniform trousers salvaged from a dead soldier, and slipped away from the wreckage and through the rice paddy that bordered the south side of the road. A hundred yards or so past the paddy, the hillside had been terraced. Then a hundred yards past the terraces the terrain rose up more steeply into a small hilltop forest.

I traveled only about three of the six miles I had planned to cover during the night. I knew I should keep moving for another hour or so to take advantage of the remaining darkness, but my gnawing belly and the knowledge that I was carrying food that would ease the pangs of hunger was more than I could resist. Mom always said food would be my downfall. Close to the top of the first hill, I found what seemed to be a good place to camp, picnic, and hide for the day.

From one of the small flat cans, I ate some of the rice seasoned with highly spiced, oily sardines. Try as I might, I couldn't get the cap off either of the beer bottles. In desperation I broke the neck off the first bottle with a rock, but that solution caused the fragile container to shatter, adding the aroma of beer to my medley of putrid odors.

The stench of the paddy water and my own stinking body didn't keep me from wolfing the food. For the remainder of the evening my stomach, which only hours ago had been rebelling from hunger, now rebelled with an intensity of indigestion and bloating such as I had never known.

Within a half-hour after I had eaten, my digestive system produced a tremendous volume of heavy gas, which soon produced a siege of belching and flatulence that I feared could be heard for a quarter of a mile and would, along with the odors, reveal my hiding place should some North Korean pass downwind within that distance.

Diarrhea and dawn arrived together. The diarrhea attack reminded me of similar attacks in the South Pacific, attacks that struck suddenly, urgently, and with demanding force. My first attempts at sanitation gave way when it occurred to me that a mere case of the "runs" could do but little, if any, damage to my personal hygiene. After all, I had spent the better part of the night crawling, sometimes neck deep, through rice paddies spiced with evil-smelling human waste, so there was nothing a simple case of diarrhea could do to further reduce my social acceptance.

The food did wonders for my morale. The continual gnawing of my empty stomach over the past days had been more debilitating than I had realized. Although the North Korean Army food subjected my alimentary canal into some digestive stress, it didn't subject my system to any more exotic peristalsis than did the menu served in the wardroom of the *Badoeng Strait*. The griping pains of the days of fasting were now gone. I felt much stronger despite the rigors of loose bowels. My muscle aches were also diminishing, and all things considered, I began to feel better about my situation.

I now knew that I had the ability to avoid capture while making my way toward freedom, and that my chances of evading the enemy increased by the hour. My confidence soared. But then the rains came.

When those first cold raindrops spattered in the dust and splashed on my face, I began an almost frantic, but eventually fruitless, search for a place that would give me some shelter. A cold front moving rapidly down through the Korean peninsula generated the rain. The mass of heavier, colder arctic air moving under the warm humid air of summer lifted it into the atmosphere where it condensed into a line of low roiling clouds that spawned an intense rainstorm.

The storms, slowed by the high mountains of Central Korea where they gathered, built enough strength to finally overpower the damming effect of the mountains. Then, renewed, they screamed across the low flat terrain.

The ascending warm air became more and more unstable as it moved higher. There, the opposing electrical differences in the towering cumulo-nimbus cloud created lightning, the accompanying thunder, and every type of precipitation known to man.

Back in survival school, the instructors emphasized the importance of staying as dry as possible. When I had zipped on my lightweight flight suit of summer Byrd cloth, five days ago, it was a warm late summer day. Now, after the five days of subjection to thorns, explosions, and tree snags, my flight suit had become ragged. Even in its tattered state it had given me some protection from the elements. But now it acted as a blotter. The best I could do for protection was to wrap myself in my blanket and hunker down with my back against a large tree trunk. Medical sources say that shivering from the cold helps the body produce some warmth, a statement I found difficult to believe as I was practically spasmodic and getting colder by the minute.

The storm wore on through the remainder of the night. I tried mind over matter and turned my thoughts to past good times, such as sitting in front of a roaring fireplace enjoying a hot Tom and Jerry while winter raged outside. I even thought of my sheltering tree being struck by a warming bolt of lightning, ever hoping that the mind over matter thing would cut in. But the cold prevailed. There was a bright side to this. At least some of the stench of the rice paddy was being washed from my body and clothing. One must always look to the bright side, more so when the brightness is by a storm in enemy territory.

Cold fronts move rapidly. They seem eager to blast their frigid discomfort upon as many humans they can as soon as possible. This one had passed before dawn, and except for the bone-chilling wind evaporating the water from my clothing, I was more comfortable. The rising sun, glinting through the streaky, post-frontal clouds, offered very little warmth, but I still needed to find a place that would offer me some shelter and concealment during the approaching daylight hours.

To continue my movement in daytime was risky. Yet I needed the activity to offset the cold. The constant loss of body heat was beginning to give me a feeling of fragility. When I finally reached the crest of the next hill I could see a small terraced space in which some form of greens was growing. Next to the flat terrace, snuggled into the edge of a small grove of trees stood a small, typical Korean farmhouse.

I lay on the wet earth for about an hour watching the hooch for any sign of activity. If anyone were at home they surely would build a fire for cooking and warmth when they awoke to begin their day's work. But the shack seemed deserted. As the daylight increased, I could see no indication of any farm animals around the hooch. At that time, rural Koreans had at least a pig and some chickens, and most had an ox, but there was no sign of human or animal activity around the hooch.

A small corral, which probably served as the night quarters of the family ox, adjoined the east side of the hooch. But I could see no ox in or around the hut, and there didn't seem to be any physical evidence of the recent presence of an ox either. Because of their genetic make-up or their diet, all oxen quickly create an environment that makes walking hazardous for anyone not shod with high-topped boots. And there was no ox cart to be seen anywhere in the area. The ox cart was the complete rural transportation system of Korea, and the absence of a cart usually indicated the absence of people.

When I finally got to the hovel, it was past mid-morning. Once inside, I began my search for anything that would be of value to my cause. I found only a small cloth bag of grain, probably food for the missing ox, and a small bundle of sticks beside the fire hearth. The sticks set me to consider building a fire, but fires make smoke, and smoke attracts people. The people most likely to be drawn to smoke issuing from an abandoned hooch would be wearing uniforms and carrying guns.

At least, the hut gave me some shelter from the cold wind, and, even without the longed-for fire, I began to feel somewhat warmer. I decided to use the shack as my hiding place during this day. Having a roof over my head for the first time in five days was comforting, even if the roof was a tattered thatch allowing occasional glimpses of the sky. My shivering had almost ceased, and I quickly fell asleep.

It was very dark when something jolted me from my sleep. I awoke shaken and confused by whatever it was that roused me from my fitful slumbers. This was neither new nor different from the feelings that assailed me every time I awoke since first being jostled awake by that NKPA captain and his huge 9mm pistol. Every awakening since my arrival in North Korea disturbed my sense of order. Sleeping through the days and staying awake at night was against my natural rhythm. I once had a tour of duty during which I flew night fighters, a time that demanded reveille at sunset and taps at dawn. During those two years I always awoke with the jitters.

The cold north wind that had been whistling through the cracks in my hooch most of the day had calmed to a breeze that moaned in a low monotone. Now instead of covering over noises with its own bluster, the low breathy moan lifted the din of an active rural countryside, and carried its voice miles from its source.

Outside the hooch, the surrounding land seemed empty. I crept out the door, and inching along in the shadows cast by the walls, I searched the night, first to the north toward the road, then around the compass in all directions, looking for some movement. It was a slow process demanding caution and requiring about an hour. My mind still dwelled on the fact that moving slowly was the single most important element of evasion. I had no idea of the hour at which I once more picked up my scant belongings and headed south. I felt a nagging reluctance to leave my shelter for which I had built a fondness during that single day.

For a change, I crossed mostly flat land, but some low hills dotted the area. One, higher than the others, stood out in the night and gave a point of reference for my march. Groves of trees covered the hills. The terrain was such that, even in the darkness, I was able to make pretty good time. The ground was covered with leaves and pine needles and an occasional fallen tree branch. But yesterday's rains had made the earth and its covering soft, which reduced the noise of footsteps.

As I moved through the woods, I began to play a kind of mind game. My thoughts galloped through the full spectrum of matters that were important to a fugitive, and I began to second-guess myself.

Perhaps I had waited too long that night before bedding down. That delay could have exposed me to capture. North Korean soldiers might even now be closing in to relieve me of my freedom, such as it was.

The spate of diarrhea had ended, thus removing much of my discomfort. And the ability to maintain a steady walking pace had warmed me considerably and eased my aches and pains. Some of these thoughts, and the feeling of satisfaction for a change, lulled me into a carelessness that compromised my safety.

The morning twilight had progressed until it was almost daylight when suddenly I realized I was walking beside railroad tracks, right out in the open, in clear view of God and any North Korean who happened to be out on a morning stroll. And there was no place to hide when a small group of NKPA troops appeared about a quarter mile down the tracks headed directly toward me.

Three trees growing close together on top of a low rise in the land some hundred yards from the tracks looked to be the only place. Could I get there before I was spotted? I cursed myself out loud for my lack of vigilance. Leonardo Da Vinci said that fear will enter the human heart faster than any other emotion. He was right! My fear of being captured at this point made my movements seem like one of those dreams when speed is required, but no matter your need, all movement seems hampered by heavy legs slogging through a sea of thick, cold molasses.

Fortunately, the soldiers were immersed in a spirited discussion. After all, they were in their home territory with no enemy airplanes around, and the day was dawning clear and brisk. They continued past the spot where I had crossed the tracks without seeing my footprints, still engaged in an animated discussion so intense as to preclude their taking notice of anything out of the ordinary.

It was almost an hour before it seemed safe to take that deep breath of relief. I made myself as small as I could and decided to spend the remainder of daylight under the scanty protection of the three trees—a less than satisfactory hiding place. But so far as I could see, they were the only protection in the featureless landscape offering any concealment. And daylight was looming.

Since that very first day of my march across North Korea, I had intended to create a means of keeping track of the passing days. I had thought that keeping some sort of calendar would be important in order to give me some sense of accomplishment as the days passed. My capture on that second day on the ground, and the following events that led to the near fatal ride in the truck had removed keeping time from my thoughts. I had, however, given it some consideration after I was freed when that Corsair blasted the prison truck back on day number two.

If I could remember the date I was shot down, I could make my calendar by whittling notches in a stick if I had a knife. But the NKPA major had taken my survival knife, and although I had secured a replacement after my liberating crash, many more urgent events kept the creation of a calendar low on my list of priorities.

The condition of the bodies of my truck guards, and those North Koreans draped about in various ghoulish positions in the convoy three days ago hadn't served to help my memory. I had seen lots of dead bodies during World War II. Those were post-rigor cases neatly laid out for the distasteful ministrations of the men of the graves registration. But fresh blood dripping from these newly created corpses with their accusing, unseeing eyes staring into eternity while their muscles still twitched with tics proclaiming their very recent demise was a completely different form of cadaver-viewing. Anyhow, no matter my neglect in keeping a calendar, I decided that today was my seventh day on the ground, and that this day would be Sunday.

Being in an airplane at ten thousand feet offered an unsurpassed panoramic view of the countryside. The pilot could see streams, rivers, railroads, highways, ox cart paths, cities, towns, and the many small villages that abounded in both of the Koreas. My memory of the topography of the country was that these villages were usually established near some source of water. This life-blood of humans and animals is also a necessary component for the existence of rice paddies.

My position atop this low hill wasn't the perfect replacement for a Corsair cockpit flying two miles above the earth, but from here, I could see a couple of miles toward the southeast. There, a small stream wended its way among the scattered rice fields.

Just before dark, I left the trees and cautiously moved toward the stream, which took me two hours, during which I endured incidents of stark terror from a close encounter with a group of North Korean civilians returning from their day's work in the fields. But after surviving the two-hours of travel, I came to the small creek. It was a sluggish stream flowing toward the west partly in the open, then through some dense undergrowth. As soon as I arrived at the stream, I filled my pilfered canteen. Then I followed the creek with great difficulty for perhaps three hundred yards, crashing my way through the undergrowth and sloshing in the cold water. Where the stream flowed along an open area, I came upon a group of eight huts clustered together on the high side of the stream bank. This sudden and unexpected appearance of the houses aroused a sense of sheer panic. I had been sloshing down the streambed without caution and blundered into a populated area!

I dropped to the ground and watched the huts for what seemed like a lifetime. As the darkness increased, no visible light, nor sound, nor movement came from the huts. But I could imagine myself moving carelessly toward the settlement and walking into a group of North Korean soldiers.

NKPA soldiers ignored these villages most of the time, except when they used them as registration points for their artillery or as hiding places to avoid Corsairs. Villagers that did catch the attention of the NKPA were assigned to onerous work details and endured the wrath of officers and NCOs who were charged with their discipline.

Civilians also stayed away from villages that were close to areas where battles would be fought should the war move into their homeland. Even the most illiterate comrade seemed to sense the approach of that peril as he watched his country's wounded soldiers fill the hospitals.

Then, too, civilians had other reasons for avoiding villages. UN aircraft had a habit of blowing these villages and huts to bits in fits of vengeance or to prevent their use by the enemy to register their big guns and mortars. A village was also a good place for pilots to get some bombing practice when they had to jettison unused ordnance on the way back home. Then there were the persistent draft details that drove about the country impressing male citizens into the armed forces. Because of these inherent dangers, refugees who were always searching for sustenance and shelter stayed away from the small villages and built-up areas.

All this was actually my own personal and private theory that I had developed while flying over the countryside since the prior August. During that time, I had rarely seen any activity around the many huts and villages, and this led me to believe in my theory and take the chance that I would find the cluster of huts unoccupied.

Though the north wind had died down considerably, the climate continued to cool. When I awoke this evening back there in the three-tree grove, there was a faint, thin dusting of frost on the ground. Winter cold would be another enemy for me to add to my growing list of bad stuff. I hadn't felt warm—really comfortably warm—since before I sat through the drenching of the cold rain that followed the passage of the cold front many hours, or was it days ago?

The village was deserted. After my lengthy surveillance I moved into the area. I combed through each hooch, carefully searching every nook and cranny, ever hoping to find something that would help me through whatever trying time I had before my rescue or capture, whichever would come first.

Rural North Koreans, which is to say the majority of the people who lived in the vicinity of the 38th parallel, placed great value on their meager belongings. When forced to leave the family farm for any reason, such as artillery bombardment, infantry fire fights, and air strikes, they packed everything movable, including such irreplaceable building materials as sheets of corrugated tin taken from their old hooch. This all went onto the family ox cart before the family began its long walk to somewhere else.

When their trek brought them to an unoccupied plot of ground that wasn't in the path of the war, they stopped, put the family ox out to graze, and began to create a new hooch with the pieces they salvaged from the last one.

This new farmland need not show great promise. Using their ancient knowledge of the land and the byproducts of both ox and family members, they seem able to extract fertility from the poorest of soils. Then, while the father constructed a family shelter, the children and the mother began the chores necessary to establish the new family farm.

First, a head or two of cabbage was shredded, seasoned with hot peppers and salt, and packed into a clay kimchi pot. A pot is sealed and buried in a spot where the sun-warmed earth will speed fermentation of the mixture. As the kimchi cooked in the warmth of its pit, a plot of land was chosen for the family garden. Then the family ox pulled the plow through the red earth to prepare a square of land for planting.

Because of the Korean penchant for salvaging useful items, I entered the first hooch not really expecting to find anything that would be of much value to a fugitive. Since ancient times, the Korean people have developed the fine art of surviving as refugees from the ravages of many battlefields. They are as renowned for leaving nothing useful behind as they are for keeping their race pure and undefiled from many invaders.

But to my surprise, in the fourth hooch, hidden under a pile of trash back in a dark, musty corner, I found a long brown woolen coat and a bundle of woolen rags. The coat was tattered and filthy with years of Korean dirt ground into the weave. It stank, exuding an aroma that reminded me of an old and flatulent bulldog a neighbor owned when I was a child. In spite of the disadvantages of odor and filth, the coat would serve to add warmth and to conceal what remained of the bright orange color of my flight suit. The rags could be used to wrap my rapidly disintegrating boondocker shoes and to blur the distinctive footprints, which bore the unmistakable sign that an American passed here. Thus, the rags served two vital purposes. Although minor, one of my growing concerns was the loss of foot covering. The heavy leather Marine Corps issue boondocker shoes had always seemed almost indestructible. But the past days of abuse and exposure had caused seams to rip, lace eyelets to come loose, and soles to separate from the welt.

In a back corner of the third hut, I was surprised to find about two quarts of grain in a small burlap sack, and glory to God, a handful of tinder inside a small tin box, and seven six-inch-long wooden matches wrapped in waxy brown paper.

My talents as a woodsman were now put to the extreme test. They almost failed. The matches were old, moldy, and damp, the moisture causing the sulfur tip to drop off the stick at the slightest touch. It was as if they had been put aside as a family treasure to be used only on special occasions, and when struck, did little more than emit a smoldering flare-up of sulfuric smoke. For more than an hour I worked with these primitive matches, drying them as best I could in the cold dampness of the hooch. I was down to the last match before I managed a small blaze in the damp tinder.

Less than an hour later I was dining on barley gruel flavored with some onion-like greens that I found growing in a small, untended garden. The temptation to get my body warm and my stomach filled had overcome my fear of being caught. When dawn interrupted my night of rest and repast, I felt somewhat renewed. For the first time since I had indulged in that stupid duel with the mountain-top machine gunner, I was really confident that I would succeed in my escape from enemy territory. Physical comfort is certainly a confidence builder.

The dawn's early light brought forth another scary episode. Although the road that passed between the huts of the village was little more than a cart path, I could hear the clanking, squeaking sound of tank wheels moving inside their caterpillar treads and the roar of a diesel engine. I used dirt from the hooch floor to smother my fire, and hoped that there was enough wind to blow any residual smoke away. As the noises came closer I chanced a quick peek outside. The tank was moving south with urgent speed across the open land. Then I saw the reason for the need for speed. He was searching for a place to hide, away from the confines of the narrow valley, where he would have the opportunity to maneuver defensively.

Four Corsairs had spotted the T-34, and were setting up for an attack. A soldier standing in the tank's escape hatch guided the driver who steered the machine. As one of the Corsairs committed for an attack, the tank made a wild turn to destroy the aim of the pilot, who pulled out of his dive for another try.

The tanker's zigzag defense, even within the narrow confines of the valley, served to spoil the first attack. Then the four planes set up in a line abreast and started their dives. No matter which way the tank turned, one of the Corsairs would be able to bring their weapons to bear. Two HVAR 5" rockets hit the tank, which stopped abruptly. Almost immediately there was a whooshing sound as its ammunition stores burned.

All this action occurred only two hundred yards from my hiding place in the village. I had seen tanks destroyed before. I had even killed a few, but this was the first time I was in a position to hear the explosions, to see the chunks of metal fly, and to smell incinerating human flesh.

The NKPA tank commander was blown through the air as a flying torch, trailing a rainbow of smoke and flame until he landed in a crumpled heap fifty feet from the flaming tank. As the flames increased in intensity, the tank's remaining stores of ammunition began to explode, looking something like a small-town Fourth-of-July fireworks display. Sparkling arcs of fire flew in all directions until the supply of explosives was expended and the flames burned away the last of the flammables.

The Corsairs searched the area for any other targets of opportunity. Finding nothing, they returned to take another look at the ruins of their killed tank. I took off the smelly coat to expose the faded orange color of my tattered flight suit, and ran waving my arms and shouting. One of the pilots saw me and flew toward my position by the village. They gave me a good buzzing, wagged their wings and turned south.

Six of the eight huts in the village bordered the narrow road, three on each side in almost military precision. The lane that passed through the village forked into a wider road that meandered off toward the northwest. This orderliness was unusual for North Korean villages where the huts were usually scattered about in a harum-scarum fashion, taking advantage of level spaces that would afford each occupant with a garden plot.

On a larger plot of land forty feet to the left of the lane, three gardens had been terraced into the west side of the low hill. This plot sat higher than the other six, and was the site of a seventh hooch that must have been the home of the village mayor or commissar, assuming these small villages had mayors or commissars.

The eighth hut was some twenty yards away from the other seven. I didn't see this shack until I had already searched through two of them. And when I saw it concealed in the trees and underbrush, I wondered why this hut was so remote from the others, standing as it was away from the village society. I also wondered if that could possibly be the resting place of some enemy soldiers.

I assumed that this had been the home of either the village grouch or a semi-hermit who valued his privacy. I decided to spend my daylight hours in the back corner of that eighth hut because of its remoteness. If it were good enough to shelter the village grouch from his fellow villagers, it was good enough to hide me from a bunch of testy North Korean soldiers.

My theory was that this more remote position would be the safest, and would allow me to hear any intruders before they could discover my presence. I decided, wisely or not, that the Corsair pilots who had killed that tank had spread the news of my position and that I should stay in the vicinity.

I managed to sleep sporadically, having dreams of that poor Korean soldier flying through the air with his body on fire. And I heard very clearly the whoosh of the HVAR's as they streaked toward the tank and the explosions when the tank went up. As I awoke for about the fiftieth time, the sun lay low in the west, deepening the shadows among the hills. Decision time had arrived once more.

I found decision-making more difficult with each passing day. Should I continue to move south, or should I stay in the vicinity? The Corsairs had seen me earlier today. Did the pilots recognize me or not? If I stayed in one place, was there a greater chance that I could be caught than if I continued to move? I never entertained the thought that the First Marine Division was beginning to rout the NKPA and chase them toward the 38th Parallel. My mind was in a messy, disorganized state. I recalled a time back on Okinawa during WWII when my squadron had been assigned to bomb and strafe anti-aircraft emplacements on the little island of Kikai in the Amami-O-Shima group. That island had been the Japanese Anti-aircraft Gunners School, and the faculty was still around.

During the first strike while I was in a dive to drop a five-hundred-pounder, one of the gunnery instructors zeroed in on my Corsair. Those bursts were popping just ahead of my plane, and I began to slow my speed. I pulled off some power at the same time the Jap slowed his traverse, and the next round got me right in the cylinders. That was the night I spent bobbing about in the East China Sea hoping the sharks wouldn't upset my raft and dine on my skinny body.

The memory of that incident where a change in tactics brought me some grief convinced me to continue my evasion efforts—to "dance with who brung me." I knew that my system was working so far, and were I to change, it might be the 1950 version of the Amami-O-Shima incident.

According to the proposed schedule of the ground forces, Seoul should have been in the hands of the UN forces by now. But schedules often go awry in wartime. Since no movement within sight or hearing had occurred since that tank had roared to its doom, I decided to rest this night where I was.

In the days before the Pusan Perimeter had been established, you could tell the enemy was moving toward you as the flood of refugees filled the roads. But none was here. For some reason I couldn't fathom, this place was in a sort of limbo. It occurred to me that I hadn't seen a bird or an animal for the past few days. I supposed that wildlife had more sense than the human race and stayed away from loud noises.

I recalled what I could of the UN timetable of advance. After much discussion with myself, I decided that it was now necessary to prepare to avoid retreating NKPA troops. I needed to find a good hiding place, perhaps on a high hill that was hard to climb, one that would offer concealment and cover.

An obstacle of this type would normally be bypassed by discouraged troops in retreat. In this situation, they would regard speed of movement to be more valuable than climbing hills. They would stay on the roads as much as possible.

The hill I finally decided upon was about three hundred meters east of the village. I estimated it to be about a hundred and fifty meters high, with a wooded area that extended across the crown of the rise. Keeping to the shadows as much as possible, I gathered my supplies, donned the filthy brown coat, and walked toward the hill. Looking back, I saw the dead tank, which the Corsairs destroyed still giving off small wisps of smoke.

At first, the climb was easy. The lower levels were terraced to create flat garden plots and had a stepped pathway that led upward from garden to garden. Soon I found that I had chosen well. After I climbed past the dirt steps, the hill became extremely difficult to scale. It took almost two hours of slipping and stumbling in the gathering darkness before I reached the summit, which was covered with a dense growth of a bristly, almost leafless shrub that grew to a height of three to four feet. A flattened area about one hundred feet square nestled beneath this scrub brush. I could move about under the foliage on my hands and knees, and from the center of the growth I could keep watch in all directions. This hill offered an almost perfect hiding place.

A number of factors affected my confidence in my ability to avoid capture, such as the approach of cold weather, the inability to sleep well during the daylight hours, and lack of food. The diminishing prospects of finding food in this war-torn land were affecting my strength. Even less important things like guessing the time of day, the number of times I had tripped and fallen during the previous night's trek all combined to build a growing doubt that I could make my way back to friendly lines.

Today I had felt a depression that set a record for an all-time high of lows. When the sun passed behind those clouds that were always on the western horizon, I lay under the brush of the hilltop, more tired, hungry and sore than I had ever been before. Sometime within the last few hours I had done something that reopened a gash on my shoulder. There was some transient pain when I moved, but my main concern was that dribble of blood and pus. My physical and mental state was such that it required extreme effort to move, and I began to worry about infection.

Chapter 15
Kill or Be Killed

It was time to begin my evening ritual of staring into the gathering darkness for signs of the enemy. I knew that I must not omit this surveillance from my routine, but my mind just couldn't seem to overcome the matter of my body's shortcomings. I stayed in my brushy hideaway for almost another hour. That delay probably saved my skin.

While my mind conquered my matter and I began to crawl out of the brushy clump, three NKPA trucks clashed their gears, drove out of a small grove of trees at the bottom of my hill, and headed south. The fact that I hadn't seen or heard them until now gave me much concern. These drivers must have been hiding in the woods all during the daylight hours as I slept, snoring and probably verbalizing my dreams only a scant fifty yards away.

I recalled that several times during the day I awoke and heard the unmistakable drone of P-51s flying over the area. And about noon, four Corsairs whistled over. Had these trucks been caught out in the open, they would now be smoldering hulks reeking with the stench of burned flesh.

That I had been spared by my delay gave my spirits a lift. I knew that feeling would continue to improve after my night's march when the new day dawned and the sunshine began to warm the earth. Then I could lay my weary bones down for a day of rest.

My wild guess regarding the military situation seemed to have been correct. Just before daylight, I was an estimated eight or nine miles south of my last resting place, and once more settling into a hiding place atop yet another hill. Before I settled down, many NKPA troops came into my view, streaming northward up the road. These troops were using every form of transportation they could find — ox carts, bicycles, motorcycles, and a few battered trucks. Wounded soldiers filled the trucks in the rather orderly convoys.

That column of retreating troops raised another possibility. Retreating troops with no means of observing the enemy often send some of their number to set up observation posts, usually on a dominant hilltop. Such an observer would have some means of communication with a rear guard, a point of security for the retreat. It was still a bit before sunrise when I heard the heavy, gasping breaths of someone climbing the hill just as I had done less than an hour ago.

In the gloom I could see the form of a man who I assumed was a North Korean. When he completed his climb, he placed his rifle on the ground and stood up, lit a cigarette, and began watching his comrades pass by on the road below.

The soldier looked to be about sixteen years old. I judged that he was five feet tall and weighed some one hundred pounds. His ill-fitting uniform was torn and dirty, his rifle had a broken stock that he had mended with rags tied around the fore-grip. He stood smoking his cigarette less than seven feet from where I was lying on my belly, scarcely daring to breathe. Standing with his back to me, he watched the pathetic retreat, occasionally glancing toward the south.

The presence of an enemy obviously prevented me from beginning my evening march, but if I stayed in the brush, he probably would see me as soon as he finished his smoke. It was time for me to decide which of us would leave this hill.

Before I attacked, I tried to remember all the survival school stuff about quick, silent kills. In the end, I remembered nothing of technique, nothing of skills learned and practiced. I knew that only one of us would leave the hilltop, and unless whatever I did was done correctly, he would be the one to climb down.

As I crawled toward the North Korean, every inch that I moved seemed to create a noise that seemed certain to alert the man who was still breathing heavily from the exertion of his climb. When I finally got near the man I leaped up from my prone position, grasped his head, and plunged my knife as hard as I could into his throat. He made a sort of whistling noise as the blade severed his windpipe. Blood gushed from his wound, and I felt its warmth and stickiness flow down my arm and onto my flight suit.

As the skies brightened, it was difficult not to look at the dead man who was still leaking blood and staring into eternity. I said a short prayer, whether for him or me, I don't know. Aviators usually fight in a clean environment where the living are left to attend the dead, as we complete our mission and return home with our hands un-bloodied and the dead and dying far below.

The NKPA soldier had a small tin of rations, a canteen full of water, his rifle, a bayonet, a blanket and four rounds of ammunition. I had already discarded one Korean rifle because I thought it would do nothing but get me killed. I believed the same thing would happen with this rifle, so I scraped a shallow hole in the ground and left the rifle and the ammunition buried under the corpse. Even though the water had a strong iodine odor and the rations were less than tasty, I added his canteen and ration tin to my pack of goodies.

As daylight came, so did the Corsairs, P-51s, and ADs. A dive for the ditches and getting as far away as they could from the targeted trucks afforded the only defense for the road-bound troops since their vehicles were easy prey to the guns of the fighters. Rockets crackled through the air, machine guns chattered, and antipersonnel bombs boomed in concert with exploding fuel tanks of the trucks. Within minutes, burning trucks, smoldering remnants of ox carts, and North Korean bodies littered the road. When the planes departed, the troops came back onto the road and continued their retreat. Few survived.

The air action over the road was heavy. I wondered why more planes weren't following the first strike to complete the carnage. Then the deep rumble of artillery fire began to vibrate along the valleys and hilltops. Help seemed to be on the way in the form of UN troops. Things were happening so fast that I didn't have the opportunity to signal any of the planes while they were busy with their killing down on the road. Then, as suddenly as they had appeared, they were gone. Only my ringing ears, the roar from the holocaust on the road, and the screams of dying men broke the silence.

As this lost opportunity began its discouraging march through my brain, a new awareness began to overcome the crackle of the burning vehicles and moans of the wounded soldiers.

At first, the noise sounded like a distant rumble of a military convoy grinding slowly up the road. Then the hum grew louder and louder, coming nearer and nearer toward my hilltop hiding place.

Chapter 16
Spotted

Between two hills, about five miles south of my position, a small dot appeared in the sky. The speck grew into the shape of an airplane, a VMO-1 from the observation squadron attached to the First Marine Division. The airplanes that flew in combat areas were military versions of airplanes built by the Convair Aircraft Company. Thousands of civilian pilots used the civilian models of such fragile aircraft both to learn to fly and to flit about the countryside on afternoons and weekends. These planes were unarmed, unarmored, and flew low and slow while the pilot served as the eyes of the ground commanders.

There was no reason that I could see for the division to send one of their planes out just to take a look at a bunch of smoldering trucks and crisply fried enemy troops. The small craft drew nearer. I could see that it was headed directly for my hill, which was probably designated Hill Number 104, the number being the height in meters of the military crest of that hill.

The VMO pilot flew directly over me as I waved and shouted. Pilots on the ground in enemy territory will always wave and shout at friendly planes as if the pilot can hear his yelling over the multiple noises an airplane makes as it moves through the air.

The VMO guy passed directly over my position and continued on his straight course for another few miles.

This was standard procedure. When an observation pilot spotted something on the ground he had to make a decision. If the sighting was of enemy troops, and the pilot took some immediate action, such as circling to affirm his sighting, the enemy would realize they had been seen.

There would be no further need for them to try to conceal their position, and all hell would break loose. The troops would begin to shoot everything they had in an attempt to destroy the small plane before the pilot could radio their position back to some cannon cockers. Artillerymen usually just wait around by their cannons, drinking coffee, polishing their guns, and listening to music broadcast by Armed Forces Radio. When someone calls in a fire mission the whole demeanor of the battery changes. Even though the men manning the big guns can't see the final results, they get their kicks when they can shoot at things and blow stuff into small pieces. This pilot must have decided that the idiot on the ground was the same dim-witted fool who had engaged in that gun-duel a week or so ago. Even though he had cost the tax-payers an expensive airplane, the miscreant should be brought back to where he belonged where he could probably be put to some use in the war.

He turned his small craft around, dived to a lower altitude, and slowed his machine to a speed just a few knots above stall. As he passed over me, he tossed a packet out the cabin window. The packet hit the ground a few yards from where I was still jumping up and down, waving and yelling my damn fool head off.

I retrieved the bundle and ripped it open to find such goodies as six K rations in their olive drab waxed boxes, a one-liter bottle of water, a sturdy survival knife (the Korean knife I had taken from the truck was still stuck in the Korean's throat) a .38 caliber Smith and Wesson revolver with fifty rounds of ammunition, three packs of Camel cigarettes, slightly smashed, and a small vial containing kitchen matches that had the striking ends waterproofed with paraffin wax.

There was a second packet inside the first, which contained a Lensatic compass, a map with my present position marked by a red dot, and the written notation, "You are here." Also marked in red were the last known positions of enemy troops, and in blue, the positions and designations of the advancing UN Forces.

When a fighting man finds himself in a position that precludes his doing what he has been trained to do and realizes he is unable to correct his situation, he may feel a deep depression. As one is stumbling about behind enemy lines, he must also deal with other emotional downers.

There is always the nagging fear that he will be caught despite his best efforts to avoid that catastrophe. He is assailed by the feeling that he has been abandoned, his situation being of much less importance than the "big picture." I spent a lot of time while trudging through the darkness fighting off the belief that the troop commanders had more important things to occupy their minds than to worry about a downed pilot. The Marine Corps always takes care of its own and never abandons the dead, wounded, or stupid. That tenet sustained me during the times of depression when I usually was able to reduce the effect of these "downers."

After finally returning to the fold, I was amazed at the breadth of the rescue effort the First Marine Aircraft Wing and the Fifth Air Force had begun minutes after I had given that hilltop machine gunner his victory. Every flight that departed the two marine aircraft carriers, the USS *Badoeng Strait* or the USS *Sicily*, were always briefed on my latest situation, possible position, and probable route of march. The Ready Room was equipped with a separate chart that had my supposed route of escape clearly marked, and my probable daily, or nightly, progress noted. Every pre-flight briefing contained the latest information on my situation, and each pilot carried an extra survival packet to drop to me if I were sighted. After that VMO pilot had risked his life to drop me the welcome packet, I began thinking that Gen. Field Harris, the wing commander, wanted me back so he could have me court marshaled for stupidity. I guess that is just how the human mind works under extreme stress.

No overpowering reason for me to abandon my hilltop hiding spot seemed necessary. Five or six hours of daylight still remained, and I engaged in a long argument with myself about not allowing new-found enthusiasm to cause me to lose my cool and do something foolish that would get me captured again and tossed back into the bed of a Korean truck. I had already expended my quota of dumb by getting into that gun-duel.

The air grew cooler. I wrapped myself in the old coat and the Korean blanket and settled down for some sleep. My confidence soared; my health seemed improved.

That map showed that I was just four miles south of Inch'on. There was still a lot of enemy territory for me to cross. The terrain between my position and what I called home was mostly rough mountainous land, crossed by deep canyons. A helicopter was the only aircraft that would be able to snatch me off a hilltop, and the choppers of 1950 had deucedly short legs. Before I would be within range of a helicopter, or close to some flat land that would allow one of the VMO planes to land and pick me out of my problems, I still had many miles to walk.

When it got light enough to see, I estimated my night's progress as being about eight miles. I made camp on yet another hilltop and enjoyed some of my rations. Hunger makes one able to enjoy K rations.

I bedded down just as the sun was painting a few red streaks in the eastern sky. It had been some time since I had gone to sleep with a full belly, and I slept soundly. About midmorning, I was jolted awake by the sound of many highflying aircraft. When I finally spotted them, I also saw a tall bank of frigid-looking clouds moving in from the northwest. Ahead of the cloudbank, a frosty ice ring had encircled the sun, reducing its heat and dimming its brightness. As the sun continued its journey across the sky, it faded and then disappeared completely behind the thickening clouds.

My nightly walk had barely begun when the north wind grew from a whispering breeze to almost gale force, and a steady rain began to pelt the dusty earth with large, cold drops. During the next hour, swirls of icy snow pellets replaced the rain, driven by high-velocity wind that tortured my exposed skin. The thin protection offered by my tattered flight suit and the rancid brown coat wasn't enough to prevent the sting of the blowing ice.

One thing I didn't need was for my footsteps to be recorded in the snow that was rapidly covering the red earth. I had walked about a mile, perhaps two, while the ever-decreasing visibility was making it impossible to stay on my course. It was time to find some protected place and dig in for the remainder of the night. Although the snowfall had become heavy enough to fill my footprints, a faint outline remained of my spoor, and across that open land my trail could be seen at the limit of visibility.

At what seemed to be about 0300, engine noises rumbled off to my right. It was impossible to ascertain in which direction the trucks were moving. After they faded away, I could hear the sound of marching troops. They were passing within a hundred yards or so of my position. I didn't take a breath as long as I could hear them. The NKPA unit was marching south.

The best I could do for shelter from the storm was to construct something from whatever was available. I used the knife from the survival kit to hack some branches from the scrawny bushes that were abundant up on the hilltop I had chosen as my stopping place. It was necessary to be careful not to cut too many branches from any one bush. Should some casual passerby see his brush destroyed, he might decide to search for the cause of the damage and find my hiding place.

I had no way of knowing whether or not the North Korean authorities had told any of the civilian population that I was still on the loose. The prevailing theory was that communist leaders would not allow that bit of information to be disseminated among the populace. Such bit of news would taint the party with a tinge of failure.

I finally managed to construct a flimsy sort of a lean-to among the other bushes under a shallow protective brow on the south side of the hill. Although it was extremely fragile, this house of sticks gave a degree of protection from the biting wind. Snow continued to fall. As small drifts accumulated, I could pack the snow between the branches, chinking some of the larger holes in my shelter.

With the overcast blotting out my "sundial," I had no idea of the time. I had succeeded in packing enough snow around the bottom of my "igloo" that, with the old coat and the blanket, I managed to achieve a degree of warmth and soon fell asleep. There was still some daylight when I awoke from a restless sleep, cold and miserable. My small part of the world was dreary, covered by the quiet whiteness of softly falling snow. The white carpet glistened and reflected the scant light, making it appear much brighter than reality. The blending of snow on the land, trees, and sky was complete, making it impossible to discern where the earth ended and the sky began.

The weather situation had precluded travel this night. The snow outside of my "igloo" was almost a foot deep and still falling. The land as far as I could see looked smooth and even, but I knew that pristine blanket concealed many pitfalls. I spent the early evening scooping snow from around the hut and packing it into crevices to seal out the frigid wind.

After about a half-hour, I had made my pile of sticks and branches into a reasonably warm igloo about three feet high and four feet in diameter. The visibility being what it was, my hiding place was almost impossible to see, even by someone passing just a few feet away.

My world was wrapped in eerie silence. As usual I began to imagine the sounds of enemy, weapons at the ready, creeping ever closer, intent on my recapture. Until now I was able to feel rather than hear the deep rumble of the war far to the south of my position. But now the war seemed to be a nonexistent thing. Thor slamming his magic hammer against the enemies of the gods could be the cause of the rumbles and "whumps" I could feel and hear. The softly falling snow damped all sound. But Thor hadn't put me here to shiver on an unnamed, remote hilltop of an enemy nation. The war wasn't a far-away affair; it was just outside the now ice-fused branches of my refuge.

I had a quick meal from a can of wieners and beans (the only C ration that wasn't frozen), followed by a mouthful of the coffee granules. Thus encouraged by food, which always revived my spirits, I decided to attempt movement. I opened the Lensatic compass, determined which way was south, then reluctantly left my semi-warm shelter.

My first step was a near disaster. I stepped on what seemed to be solid, snow covered ground only to discover the snow was a deep drift that covered a drop-off of some six feet. I tumbled about a hundred feet down the hillside before crashing into a clump of brush that stopped my fall.

A tentative self-examination proved I was all right, except for some additional sore spots. If that sliding fall didn't arouse any unfriendly people, I probably could move without increasing the danger of being caught. I noticed that the heavy snowfall was beginning to cover the ground I had swept bare during my fall. Perhaps it would cover the trail of footprints that I would leave as I walked along, always moving south. As long as the snowfall was heavy enough to cover these tracks, it was possible to move with some degree of safety.

Maintaining a course in the snow was difficult. I referred to the compass frequently, checking my course about every one hundred yards. I found that even in the space of a few minutes I could become completely turned around, a situation that made using the compass difficult. By the time I could finally get my cold-benumbed hands to open the sights, the falling snow would cover and frost the lens. After a while, I got smart enough to operate the Lensatic while holding it under my blanket.

This process continued for about four hours when the cold and the diminishing snowfall forced me to discontinue travel. I began my usual pre-dawn search for a hilltop place to hole up for the daylight hours. I was still convinced that hilltops were the safest places to spend this time. Hillsides always seemed to offer shallow caves and overhanging caprock ledges in some abundance. On the west side of the slope of one of the low hills, I found just such a ledge. It was a thick slab of shale-like stone that had defied the erosion of the spring rains.

Perhaps some sort of animal had burrowed into this space, digging away the earth from under the stone, and creating the shallow cave. However it had been done, the opening under the rock was large enough for me to crawl out of sight about four feet back under the slab of rock and far enough to shelter me from the arctic snow and wind.

Before I departed the "igloo" last evening, I had placed some of the K rations inside my flight suit. I knew the exertion of the hike could increase my body heat and thaw the food. I dined on some crackers and a can of lima beans and ham, which were absolutely last on my list of preferred K ration meals. The beans in a tin of lima beans and ham resembled lima beans in shape only. The ham consisted of minute squares of the meat, and all had been reduced to pulp by whatever process was used to place a portion into an olive drab can. The green lima beans were always faded into an unappetizing yellowish shade, which matched the bleached-out chunks of ham. The tiny ham hunks looked to be somewhat smaller than peas, and made me longingly remember those huge slices of ham served aboard the ship. But looks are deceiving. No matter what the label said of the contents, all had the same, distinctive distaste of K rations. The aroma of the food mingled with some faint, musky animal odors of the cave.

The cave was warm, my stomach was satisfied, and I felt reasonably comfortable considering my circumstance. One thing that was necessary before sleeping was to prepare the earthen "mattress." Before I wrapped myself in the tattered remnants of the old brown coat and rolled myself up in the blanket, I spent a few minutes removing some rocks and rearranging the dirt so that I might have depressions in the soil where I had humps in my body. In the forests I could always pad the ground with leaves and pine needles, but here, only a thin carpet of powdery soil covered the hard-packed dirt. Sound sleep was a vital necessity to get me through my nocturnal hike, so I needed the most comfortable bed possible.

Some time passed before I achieved a semblance of comfort. While working to improve my bunk of the day, and before I gave in to fatigue, a new and disturbing thought suddenly entered my mind with a strength that relegated my desire for survival into some minor niche in my brain. Almost a week had passed since that North Korean lad had won the gun duel. By now my wife had probably received the telegram declaring me to be "missing in action" and had visited my parents to relay the message.

In December, my wife and I would reach the fourth anniversary of our wedding. Carrier deployments had caused us to be separated on two of the three previous anniversaries, and I prayed that I would not miss the fourth while stumbling about North Korea as an MIA.

I recalled the anguish my mother felt when I went to war eight years ago. Mom had resisted my enlistment as long as she could, but finally agreed to sign the papers after my draft notice arrived in the mail.

My older brother was already away at war as a crew-member of a battleship, and Mom was reluctant to have both her boys in harm's way. Now she had seen that telegram and was suffering the pain mothers feel, and I was unable to tell my family that I was alive and, so far, free. I could picture my dad, stoic and calm, puffing at his old briar pipe while he grieved.

How could I counter that message? Perhaps one of my squadron mates would call my wife with the news that I was still running free and moving toward friendly lines. I had never had much use for ESP or mental telepathy, so I decided to try prayer. For the first time since my attack of stupidity, I felt a twinge of sorrow for allowing my desire to escape to erase all thoughts of my loved ones and their anguish.

Just three feet away, the moaning winds, and the soft rustle of snow falling on winter-crisp leaves covered any night sounds. I felt safe and secure in the thought that no one would be wandering about in this weather, except, perhaps, the wild animals that had inhabited this cave before I came. I fell asleep thinking of my family.

During these days of my servitude in the limbo of North Korea, one thing continued to nag at me and thus cause me much concern. I really didn't know why. Hell, I wasn't sure of the day of the week, but not knowing the time of day really bugged me. During our short passage through life, we tend to measure everything we do by seconds, minutes, hours, days and years. Time is of no importance to God, who I am sure, was satisfied with His creation of the movements of the earth, sun, and moon. He had spoken the words, "Let there be light," and these elements obeyed the command to make the light and darkness.

Then Man began to fiddle with things like the hourglass and moon phases, and eventually created the calendar. He persisted in this obsession with the whole concept of the passage of time, and finally invented the clock. This act placed the human being who was without a timepiece at a disadvantage. Without that clock, he doesn't know when to get into the car and drive to meet his wife for lunch, or the precise moment that he should walk into the board room for an important conference that will enhance his career. Both men and women have a need for a watch and expect chaos without it. Often the last part of a man's obituary states the year he was brought into the world, and his death certificate states the minute he departed.

I had not known the exact time since that Korean had taken my watch from me back on my second morning on the ground. I was fully accustomed to wearing that Hamilton since I purchased it from the marine quartermaster back in 1942. Its loss forced me to estimate the hours from the position of the sun in the sky.

Even under the most ideal circumstances my ability to act as a human sundial left much to be desired. Now, since these thick clouds obscured the sky, and snow covered everything else, I hadn't the faintest idea of the time of day, only that it was day or night.

Clocks have ruled military men, even more than civilians, almost since the clock was invented. Everything the military does is done when some clock indicates the specific time that has been set for a specific action. Every evening the navy prints and doles out a publication they call "The Plan of the Day." This is a sheet of paper that leaves no part of any day to chance. The Plan of the Day states the times that the items of tomorrow's routine are to begin, such as the time to wake, to eat, to work, to go to sleep, and even the time to sweep the decks aboard ship. Each action is laid out on the POD.

At this time in my career, I had been in the Marine Corps for more than eight years. I entered the service, as a gawky, green college sophomore who hadn't a vague idea about his future just after the Japanese had done their nasty thing at Pearl Harbor. During these past years, I had helped fight WWII and had advanced to the rank of captain in the regular United States Marine Corps. I had gotten a mission for my life.

Since that first day as an aviation cadet, my life was pretty much governed by clocks. During my youth, radio stations would broadcast the "time signal" each day at noon to allow Man to set himself right with the sun. The government had the most accurate clocks in the whole world and fully expected its citizens to take advantage of them.

Now, in what I truly believed was the greatest crisis of my life, I didn't have a watch. Even though the lack of an accurate indication of the minutes and hours of each day bugged the hell out of me, that fact didn't make one bit of difference. The only indication of time that mattered in my situation was whether it was daylight or dark, whether I should rest in some hiding place, or walk closer to freedom. I did know that it was day twelve of my debacle and that I had many miles to go before I would be once more in the bosom of the corps.

The sounds of war in the distance jarred me awake about two hours before sunset. The noises were those dull, far-away vibrating sounds made by artillery pointing in your direction. The sounds seemed to be getting nearer and nearer, stirring the quiet evening air into waves that rippled through the trees on my hilltop hideaway. The thumps reminded me of some vague echoes resounding from noise made by someone in a narrow canyon who cared little for quiet.

Closer war noises are sharp, palpable crackling sounds that sting and make your eardrums ache. These were sounds made by the heavy caliber guns that were so far in the distance that the cracking sharpness died away in the insulation of dust and air. The volume of the rumbling indicated that there was a major offensive underway. How far away? Twenty, fifty miles? There was no way for me to tell. Explosions of military magnitude have a tendency to reverberate along the walls of valleys and canyons for great distances.

My ability to estimate the time of the day was improving, or so I thought. I knew it was late in the day. Greatly dimmed by the icy looking clouds, the sun shone slantingly on the rapidly melting snow.

My little cave under the rock ledge was warm and snug. The animal odors and odors from the lima beans and ham had been replaced by the less-than-aromatic rankness of my body. It was the first time I recall ever having been able to smell myself. There is a distinctive aroma that hangs about a group of soldiers in combat. This is a conglomeration of odors that contain the stench of unwashed bodies, spent gunpowder, the various oils and greases of machinery, plus that disturbing and acrid tang of expelled body gases.

The warmth under there, and the frigid look of the open terrain, fostered the temptation to stay put and rest for another day. My food supply was adequate for my needs, and water wasn't a problem because I hadn't felt thirsty while trudging through the cold and snow during my last nocturnal walk. I had consumed only a third of the water in my bottle. At this rate, the flask would last for two more days. Perhaps I would come upon some source of drinkable water before exhausting my supply. Surely I could melt some snow.

I broke my fast with the last of the Korean rice and sardines, my only remaining food since I had eaten the packet of crackers from the K rations some time back. Physical stamina was important, even more so since I seemed to be close to the battlefront.

A Marine Corsair offers close support to ground units brought in close contact with the enemy. The plane zooms skyward through the smoke after dropping Napalm on a Red concentration. Note flame at base of hill below plane.
Photo courtesy of the Naval Institute Photographic Collection

I assumed that the First Marine Division would be in the lead during the move out of Seoul, and marines always preferred to lead the way for the advancing grunts with a lot of Corsairs dropping bombs and other explosive devices. After ending the close air support, the Eleventh Marine Regiment, the cannon cockers of the division, would continue the bombardment with a walking barrage ahead of the leading infantry unit that would "be leaning into its supporting fires" and moving forward while the stunned enemy soldiers were still hugging the bottoms of their foxholes.

This assumption turned out to be false. The marines, after securing the city of Seoul, had been pulled from the line and were boarding ships to sail to Wonsan on the east coast of the peninsula, where they would make an amphibious landing and proceed up the spine of the country to the Yalu River.

I would need all the stamina I could muster to survive the approach of UN Forces. It was possible that I would soon find myself trapped between opposing forces, enjoying the effects of bombardment from each. Perhaps the heavy snowfall would be the least of the perils facing my continued efforts to escape.

But then the snowfall ceased. The wind shifted around to the east and blew a little warmth into my cave. When I next awoke it was dark and clear. The snow had melted except in places shaded from the prior day's feeble sunshine, little corners of earth that glistened in the dim starlight.

Outside my cave, the atmosphere was one of Indian summer, clear and warm. When the evening twilight ended and the sun sank farther below that bank of clouds that habitually hung over the horizon, deepening the shadows, I began my usual trek.

Back in survival school, there was an instructor worthy of recall. Amazingly, this educational experience of more than two years ago had been etched into my mind more deeply than I thought. This instructor was an Army Air Corps fighter pilot who had been shot down over France during the early days of the United States' involvement in WWII. This was in mid-1942, and the French underground was still in its rudimentary stages, but with their help, he managed to walk to freedom.

Upon his return to Britain, he was asked to return to France and work with the underground to organize an escape system for American and British pilots. He spent two years at this duty and was instrumental in the escape of many downed pilots and crewmen.

After the Normandy landings, the situation became so fluid that this underground-communications expert was unable to cope with the rapid changes. He was captured by the Nazis, and was enroute to Berlin for deep interrogation when the train was strafed and wrecked. He killed his Nazi escort, and while using the dead Nazi's SS uniform, was captured by the Russians in Berlin. His final wartime coup was to escape from Russia and to return to the USA. The air force had either to commit him to an asylum or use him to teach survival. They chose the latter.

His continuing mantra was, "Never, never give up, and always keep your thoughts on your goal." He also told us that after an escapee had evaded capture for a week or so, especially when the tactical situation was fluid, the enemy had turned to more pressing needs and had probably given up the hunt. The escapee would then have become a forgotten piece of wartime flotsam.

The importance of recapturing an escapee would have been diminished as units were shuffled and assigned different zones of responsibility. In addition, it was entirely possible that the few North Koreans who knew an American aviator was loose in their country, and still had an interest in his recapture, were lying dead and cold in a paddy somewhere.

This information from long ago came back to me in bits and dabs during my days of struggle. Occasions would arise that would let me recall little things that are important for a successful evasion. These mind exercises helped to dispel the fear and the loneliness and did much to fend off depression and doubt.

I had almost decided that the North Koreans no longer cared about capturing me. They had serious problems with the huge UN forces and were no longer able to spare men to make organized searches for a single pilot. Common-sense thinking would come to the conclusion that the downed aviator had either been killed or had starved to death. The feeling that I was not being tracked down was comforting. Then another really big problem flared up.

Chapter 17
Up Close With The Enemy

About a half-mile north of my small hiding place several large NKPA units appeared, including T-34 tanks and about fifty trucks carrying troops. As soon as they arrived, about five hundred men scurried about the hillside preparing defensive positions. One group was filling sandbags, another digging fighting pits in the hillside, and others were laying land mines in every part of the land that could be traversed by vehicles. Machine gun crews prepared positions for their guns and anti-tank weapons, and engineers began felling trees to clear fields of fire.

Enemy soldiers spread out over the hillside and down into the valley facing toward my little hill, which might soon be occupied as an observation post. I assumed that, at best, I would soon be sitting between two opposing military units doing a lot of shooting at each other. My survival training did not cover this contingency. Then my mind began to play some tricks with my body. That old depression demon returned when I realized that I was sitting between a rock and a hard place with little chance of getting out of the trap unobserved.

The weather had chipped in with a new spasm of Mongolian atmospherics, and the snow returned. I was amazed at how fast the clouds rolled over the land and how the brutally strong north winds scoured the hillsides. Before darkness settled in, snow, sleet, and freezing rain once again added to my misery.

I knew that weather guessers possessed a huge vocabulary of descriptive words to relay their theories about the causes of these atmospheric phenomena. These words and phrases did nothing but confuse the uninitiated about what was happening in the sky.

Precipitation was one of their words that covered a multitude of stuff, and all of it seemed to be falling along with my spirits. The remainder of my meteorological knowledge served me naught. It was cold, raining, and snowing, and the atmospheric reasons for this were unimportant to me.

None of the very competent instructors in escape-and-evasion school had ever given any instructions about what to do when faced with the situation that confronted me.

I was hiding on a low hill that appeared to be directly between UN Forces invading the Koreans' country, and a large force of NKPA troops who were becoming more and more desperate to defend their land. These two foes had very few options. So did I.

Several hours remained before it would be dark enough to move without being seen. I adopted the rule: When you can't do something constructive, don't do anything. I sat and watched.

When the shadows of the night deepened, and I felt it was safe, I moved down the side of my hill as quietly as I could and departed the area as fast as prudence would allow. Snow, rain, strong winds, and spates of sleet made five-hours of walking through strange countryside a time of torture. Just before daylight, I found an almost secure spot to spend my day. I had spent most of yesterday being afraid to sleep, watching the panorama of the NKPA troops in their almost frantic haste to prepare a defense. The effects of increasing cloud cover had made the daylight pass much faster than it ever did when I was alone out in the woods just waiting for the gathering darkness to cover my movements. I left my hiding place just as the mine-laying detail was moving toward the road that passed the foot of "my" hill.

After about four hours of stumbling and slipping, I estimated that I had covered almost three miles. I could no longer hear the North Koreans, so that eerie silence of loneliness once more wrapped me in its blanket. As I walked along a level area, I began a weird bit of philosophical musing. I had enjoyed watching the Koreans in their labors. It was like having company in the house, a personal entertainment system. Time had somehow left me feeling rested even though I had missed my sleep.

The increasing cold became more of a factor affecting my survival. Another concern was my rapid loss of strength and body weight. When I was shot down, I carried one-hundred-sixty pounds on my five-foot-nine-inch frame. By now, all of my excess fat was gone. My ribs were beginning to protrude, and my knees and ankle joints had become larger and swollen. My skin, relieved of the tightening effect of muscle and fat, was now much too large to fit snugly over my muscle and bones. I had developed the neck wattles of an old man, and my diminishing stamina and strength increasingly concerned me.

My once bright orange-colored flight suit had become a grimy, smelly, dingy, brownish color. The navy makes these aviation-style rompers in small, medium, and large sizes. Each size is equipped with tabs and buttons designed for waist size adjustment. When I had departed the USS *Badoeng Strait*, my waist tabs were buttoned to accommodate the maximum girth afforded a medium size suit. As I traveled, the suit had become more ill fitting until the waist tabs were cinched up to the smallest size. It was still too large, even before the buttons had given way to rot and had dropped off. Rice paddy water corrodes whatever it touches with amazing speed. I once drove a jeep through paddy water and witnessed major corrosion just two days later.

When I decided there was no market for this type of diet regimen, I put it out of my mind. Being somewhat assured that there were no NKPA folks ahead of me, I became bolder and stepped up my pace. This soon proved to be a poor decision.

There were no trails or paths along the route I had chosen. Although I was moving more toward the narrow coastal plains of the western peninsula, there were still many hills to cross. While moving down the south slope of a low hill some time after midnight, I stepped into a snowdrift that served to cover a drop-off about five feet high. The fall wasn't so much, but the landing was a bummer. I landed heavily on my left ankle and felt a searing pain stab up my leg.

Everyone has a part of his body that seems always to bear the brunt of that person's clumsiness or carelessness. For me, it was my left ankle, the same one I tore up back in early 1942 while attempting to beat the record by running the obstacle course at the Athens Georgia Preflight School. Since that time if ever I were to suffer leg injury, it would be that ankle. And so it was once more. Hunger, thirst, fear, pain, and loneliness—each of these has some effect on escape and evasion. But the escapee can overcome these things. He believes he is going to make it, and this creates a positive state of mind, a determination to complete the task at hand.

Physical injury is another story. My left leg wouldn't support my weight without great pain. A broken arm would be no more than one hell of an inconvenience, but my legs had been and still remained my only form of transport. By my own estimation, I still had perhaps fifty miles to cover before I could find safety. It was splint time.

Twenty-odd years before, when my ambition was to become a qualified life guard, one of the major requirements was the successful completion of the Red Cross First Aid Course. During this training, one of the techniques taught was the care and splinting of broken bones.

During naval aviation training, first aid instruction was eliminated to reduce training time because of the ever-increasing demand for qualified aviators. When I first injured my ankle in '42, there were medical corpsmen who took charge of the injury, gave me a couple of APC tablets, a pair of crutches, a slip of paper that allowed me to ride to my destinations, and a pat on the back. When the throbbing ankle kept me from sleep the first evening, I unwrapped their ACE bandage and hobbled along as best I could until I was released to the tender mercies of the school football coach.

It was assumed that a marine injured or wounded on the field of battle would be cared for by corpsmen. Whether anyone in high places had ever given a thought to a marine in my precarious position, I didn't know and had never asked. At any rate, I spent the rest of the dark hours and most of the next day in a small clump of trees, trying and testing a variety of splints and wrappings made from available sticks and strips of cloth from that dirty old coat. The whole exercise was one of finding a combination that would allow me to walk over rough ground with the least amount of pain.

Although my daytime hiding spot wasn't very secure, I decided to forgo any attempt at movement that night. While resting, I finished off the remainder of my food supplies and water. The next night I would have to move on.

I spent the whole day nursing my sprained ankle and watching the countryside. It was hard to believe a nation engaged in a war with armies from almost every country of the United Nations could have large areas so devoid of people. During the daylight hours, I saw seven North Koreans moving south accompanied by two ox carts, their chickens, a pig, and some material for building a new home. A few hours later, two decrepit Korean trucks filled with what appeared to be wounded men rattled and coughed down the road. After the itinerant Koreans with their ox carts and trucks bearing the wounded soldiers had passed from my field of vision and range of hearing, the countryside was empty and desolate once more.

The night crept slowly over the land to end that cold fall day. Approaching the point of fatigue, I dreaded the coming darkness. I knew nightfall was the time to resume my march south, and even discounting an extremely sore ankle, I dreaded the exertion of the hike. I reminded myself that, although I was damned tired and getting hungry again, I didn't care to take a rest period in a North Korean or Manchurian POW camp. A mild wind from the east wafted a chill through the dry air, while light from the almost-full moon in a clear sky seemed almost as bright as the pale sun had been during the day.

My ankle had swollen to monumental size. As the swelling increased so did the throbbing pain. Last night, I had found it necessary to remove what was left of my shoe in my attempt to ease the pain. Now that it was once more time to be on my way, I couldn't get the shoe back on. I removed the filthy ankle wrappings again. They had been removed and re-wrapped so many times during the past twenty odd hours that the cloth was becoming even more frayed and twisted. It took me about an hour of re-wrapping the cloths to support my ankle so as to replace my shoe and to put weight on the injured ankle.

I whittled a stout branch from one of the trees into a semblance of a walking stick. Then gritting my teeth, I began my delayed journey. The going was slow, a battle of will power over pain. Or perhaps it was the drive resulting from pure fear of being caught that gave me the endurance. Anyway, I managed about three miles before I found it necessary to take a rest within the shadows of a grove of trees.

My hunger and thirst once more began to demand attention. For the past few days, I had crossed no running creeks or rivers, nor any other source of water to replenish my canteen. Water was more important than food, so I hobbled around among the trees, hoping to find one of those small springs dripping from the ever-present rocks. I found nothing. Since the intense cold prevented me from filling my canteen with melted snow, I resigned myself to eating some snow even though it hurt my teeth.

But my search turned into a blessing in disguise. While in the deeper part of the woods, I could hear the rattle and crunch of soldiers on the move. In a few minutes, I could see a party of about twenty North Koreans moving southward. This group appeared to be a scouting patrol that had been sent out to reconnoiter enemy positions. Oddly, they had sent no men to point their march. I waited and watched, maintaining silence in the expectation that this small unit would at least have some men out to their flanks. For a recon unit to be walking along in a group with no point men or outriders told me that they didn't expect to meet any enemy in the near future. They were too involved in marching through the darkness to notice me in the shadows of the trees only some twenty yards away.

The group was out of my sight around yet another hill when all hell broke loose in spades. It seemed that the North Koreans had run face to face with a UN group with the same mission. A fierce firefight destroyed the quiet of the early morning. The "Land of the Morning Calm" became the "Land of the Morning Chaos," as the crack of M-1 rifles and the rumble of a BAR destroyed both the calm of the night and most of the enemy.

There was no way that I could move fast enough to get close enough to that UN patrol to signal to them. I had to wait up on the hill until I was sure that the surviving North Koreans had retreated past my position. I hoped that the UN patrol would continue their search to the north and that I could move close enough to the site of the firefight to make them aware of my plight without getting shot.

Presenting a target to a group of soldiers who have just survived an unexpected encounter with an enemy, and who still have great gobs of adrenalin coursing through their veins, and their rifles "loaded and unlocked," seemed just plain dumb.

Whoever the UN patrol was, they had found the enemy and had probably radioed to their main unit that the foe was capable of resistance. That done and duly reported, a scouting patrol, especially one with casualties, is usually recalled, so I never even came close to a visual contact that could have taken me out of harm's way.

Those pink first lights in the eastern skies that signal the approaching dawn, were lightening before I could move with any feeling of security. I had just emerged from the trees when I heard that most welcome sound of Pratt-Whitney R-2800 Corsair engines.

That patrol probably had called in the news of the first enemy contact, and the Tactical Air Support Center had launched a mission. As the planes came closer I could also pick out the lesser noise of one of VMO's small observation planes.

The Corsairs flew past at about ten thousand feet. At their altitude, they could neither see my feeble waving nor hear me yelling myself hoarse for their attention. But that VMO pilot was flying at about five hundred feet and must have seen my cavorting at the edge of the trees because he suddenly turned and flew directly toward my position.

Then it became evident that the Corsairs were flying cover for the VMO whose apparent mission was either to drop more supplies or to rescue me.

VMO pilots have a thing about landing their small planes almost anywhere. I had seen them land safely on hillsides where the slope of the ground seemed excessive for safety and should have been aerodynamically impossible. I had seen one VMO pilot land his plane on a rubble filled street back in Inch'on to pick up a badly wounded marine. I watched with relief and fascination as this pilot plopped his craft down on an ox path at the foot of the hill.

Convair OY-2 Sentined from Marine Observation Squadron 6 (VMO-6), 1951

The pain and discomfort of my ankle didn't slow me as I raced down the hillside and clambered into the rear seat of the OY-1. Long experience had already taught me that the fortunes of war could turn either favorable or disastrous in an instant. But the abruptness of my rescue from fugitive to freedom astonished and overwhelmed my senses for quite some time. Before I was completely settled, the pilot was turning his plane and adding power for his take-off run back down the ox path, impelled by the knowledge that NKPA troops were only a few kilometers distant. I watched the trees flash by with a detached fascination. I had a weird thought that we would never get off the ground and through the act of saving me from the North Koreans, this guy was going to get me killed.

When the plane was safely airborne, the pilot turned around in his seat, shook my hand, and asked me to please open the window for some fresh air. One of the greatest blessings in ground combat is that everyone around you exudes the same degree of odor and rankness, so no one notices. But to be in the confines of a small, cramped cockpit is another thing. My stench was unbearable to someone like my rescuer had showered within the past week and needed the fresh air to clear the vile aroma out his airplane. But the cold air blasting through the open window brought on a new almost uncontrollable spasm of shivering. I thought of closing the window and asking the pilot for more cabin heat. On second thought, I decided that heat really wasn't as important as dissipating the odors I had brought aboard. I was going home, a knowledge that rang in my ears and made the cold seem very comfortable.

Chapter 18
Return to the Fold

The flight back to what passed for civilization in that section of Korea required a few minutes over an hour. Initially, the dusty green and dingy atmosphere that battle smoke gives to the landscape masked the area. Everything we could identify through the pall had a surreal appearance of being just far enough away to be unreachable.

After thirty minutes in the air, we had passed south of the active fighting zone, and the air cleared somewhat. The wind was still blowing softly from the north, and some of the misty-looking haze dulled the land, limiting visibility to about five miles. Once we had arrived in the clearer air, the pilot was able to follow the main highway from P'yŏngyang to Seoul. The road was filled with UN vehicles, all moving northward.

My rescuer was the same Lt. Morency that had dropped the supplies to me some days earlier. Now that aerial navigation was easier in the clearer air, Morency began to shout the latest news to me over the engine noises.

He told me that, for the past three days, resistance had almost ceased, and the NKPA, except for some by-passed troops who were still fighting, was almost completely defeated. The NKPA units were retreating into the rugged mountains and the high plateau of North Central Korea. The retreat had become a rout.

The ROK Capitol Division was driving up the east coast of the peninsula as fast as their vehicles and the fuel resupply could afford. The ROKs were keeping to the road in their pell-mell advance, leaving large pockets of by-passed enemy troops for others to clean up. They moved with the belief that a rapid arrival at the Yalu River would bring an end to the fighting and a reunification of the nation.

The First Marine Division had been pulled from the lines and was back aboard ships from which they would make another amphibious landing somewhere on the east coast. After the landing, they would be prepared to move to the north until the diplomats could negotiate an end to the war.

Those words made me cringe with the thought that this war would drag on and on while those diplomats from both sides argued about petty details that were almost impossible to resolve, as hundreds of soldiers still died in battles being fought to enhance the diplomatic position.

I was still munching on some K ration crackers and cheese, the only food aboard that my sore teeth could tolerate, when we suddenly banked steeply and began a landing approach to a short, narrow airstrip beside a group of tents marked with huge red crosses.

At the end of our landing roll, I was helped from the rear seat of the plane, placed on a litter that smelled of blood, and carried into one of the tents. I could hear the engine of Morency's airplane rev up and then fade as it increased the distance on another take-off.

I never had the opportunity to express my gratitude to Morency. When I was back on flying status more than a month after my rescue, I flew a Rescue Combat Air Patrol over a downed VMO pilot who had been flying up a canyon at dusk. He had flown into some electric transmission cables and crashed into the rugged terrain south of the Chosin. Killed in the crash, Morency's body was never recovered.

An army medic began the noxious chore of stripping away my clothing. An orderly helped me to a small shower tent a few feet away. He gave me a bar of soap, a bottle of some green liquid and a washcloth, and told me to scrub hard. The water was hot and plentiful, and I took luxurious advantage of both the soap and the hot shower. After a few minutes, I began to feel warmth creep back into my bones, a delicious feeling. And as I watched the dirt from my body mixed with the soapy residue of cleanliness swirl down the shower drain, I began to take stock of my condition.

During my time evading North Koreans, I had lost almost twenty percent of my body weight. My ribs stuck out and my knees and elbows appeared to be swollen when compared with my skinny arms and legs. My still swollen ankle appeared grotesque, my toes black and pudgy. After I finally felt clean, two of the doctors examined me and found me in "surprisingly good condition." I weighed in at one hundred twenty pounds—down about forty pounds, much of which was muscle loss. After the examination, I was led to a clean bed and told to rest while some army medical corpsmen placed IV drips into both my arms.

An army man brought a tray with a glass of milk, several glasses of assorted juices, two pieces of toast, and a bowl of clear broth that smelled of spices and garlic. I downed the milk, took two or three spoons of the broth, and a nibble of the toast before an overwhelming fatigue swept me into sleep.

Later, I was told that I slept soundly for twenty hours. I also learned that my return to the fold had been duly reported to the captain of *Badoeng Strait*, the Marine Aircraft Command at Kimpo, and the Fifth Air Force. More importantly, word of my rescue had been sent to my wife who would have to await some recuperation and debriefing before getting a call from me, probably through a ham radio operator.

I awoke with a ravishing hunger but with a digestive tract that just couldn't seem to become used to real food. My first meal of solid food stayed with me for all of ten minutes before I vomited it, along with a goodly dollop of blood, into a stainless steel basin. It was back to the liquids for another day, then a tea-and-toast routine for two days more, and finally some meals of obnoxious-looking pureed vegetables. On the fifth day, the doctors decreed that I could have solid food in the form of coddled eggs.

Although Korean farmers always seemed to have a flock of chickens about, our eggs normally came as powder from a box and were mixed with water then scrambled. After powdered eggs have been cooked and placed on a plate, that water seems to re-constitute itself into a pale yellow juice that just weeps across the plate. Powdered eggs cannot be coddled no matter the talents of the cook.

But somehow the doctors had found a supplier of real eggs encased in real shells. Brown or white, they were small, but all freshly snatched from the biddy's nest.

The first time I was allowed to leave my bed and walk to the hospital mess, the cook, the same man who had been sending me goodies as I lay abed, asked me if I felt able to eat some real fried eggs. Within minutes I was served a plate that held four eggs, sunny side up, and a thick, juicy slab of rare beefsteak. Heaven had come down to Korea.

I endured five more days of every test known to medical science and a full day of debriefing by those who believed my experience would benefit other unfortunates. During this time I ate, slept, and had my temperature and blood pressure taken at all hours of the day and night. Finally, the medics pronounced me fit enough to be released to the evacuation hospital.

I was flown back to Itami where I was to take my rest at the Takaraska Hotel, a paradise snuggled among the hills above the Itami Air Base. The Takaraska Hotel was one of many small resort hotels that the occupation forces had commandeered after the signing of the surrender accords back in 1945. Like all the others, the Takaraska was then the epitome of Oriental luxury. The hotel amenities included tennis courts, workout facilities, and above all, those delicious hot baths and a cadre of masseuses who could put anyone to sleep.

The bar was stocked with an ample supply of American and Canadian whiskeys, splendid wines and liquors, and everything else, except good Scotch whiskey. The substitute for the Scotch was a Japanese concoction distilled by the Suntory Distillers, and referred to as Scotch, which it surely wasn't. But, as they say, after one has imbibed three or so of anything, the hint of peaty barley malt isn't missed, and it all tastes good.

Two days after I arrived at the Takaraska Hotel, the pilots from one of the MAG 12 squadrons came to enjoy an R and R respite from the fighting in Korea. These marines were all aware of my trials and tribulations in the hills of Korea, and I was amazed when each of these men professed that he had seen me on the ground.

I was summoned to Itami on the fourth day of my Rest and Recreation. Major General Field Harris, the commanding general of the First Marine Aircraft Wing, wished to have a chat about my experience. He had read all the debriefing reports and said he would like to hear the real story. We talked for an hour after which he pinned a Bronze Star Medal and a Purple Heart onto my shirt, shook my hand, and told me to hurry back to my squadron.

Two weeks of doing nothing can become boring. After the first week, I asked to return to the squadron. Arnie

Lund, the skipper, wanted me to fly some field-carrier landing practice flights at Itami to make sure I could still manage to get a Corsair onto the boat. After two days, the wing LSO pronounced me qualified, and the next morning I flew aboard the *Badoeng Strait*. It seemed like yesterday. I had a "roger pass" and caught the third wire.

The flight schedule for the next day had me leading a RECCE on the "cannon ball run," which covered the main roads from the Chosin to the Yalu and return. Buck would be flying on my wing. He had condescended to fly another mission with me only after I swore with my hand on the squadron SOP that I would not engage in gun dueling, no matter who shot at me.

Chapter 19
Aftermath

I was privileged to fly seventy-six more missions before I received orders back to the States. Soon after the U. S. Marine Division fought its way off the Chosin Plateau, it was moved back to the old bean patch in the Masan area for refitting. The U.N. forces on the peninsula finally stopped the Chinese advance, and all units began a period of rebuilding.

I was transferred to Wing Operations as Assistant G-3. My collateral duty was to serve as General Harris' pilot until the end of May 1951. The diplomats of the UN and other interested countries began to foster a peace commission in late 1951. Delegates were chosen, and these began negotiations in a place called Panmunjom. While men died, these so-called peacemakers haggled for months over such vital points as the size and shape of the conference table. They finally agreed on the height of the flagpoles as more men died. The solution as to the menu to be served the negotiators was finally resolved, while men died trying to take and hold hill 213. Finally, after months of discussions, a cease-fire was proclaimed and quiet reigned over "The Land of the Morning Calm." Then the POWs came home.

In 1960, I was assigned to VMF 235 stationed at MCAS Beaufort, SC. The squadron participated in the Bay of Pigs operation and the evacuation of Americans from the Dominican Republic after the assassination of its dictator.

On the last day of February 1963, I stood at attention and watched the band from Parris Island march by playing the "Eyes of Texas" at my retirement parade. My wife and

I drove through the main gate at MCAS Beaufort, South Carolina, at noon and arrived three days later in Texas.

After my retirement, I worked as an independent flight instructor. When my medical clearance had expired, I was forced to have a qualified pilot with me in the cockpit of the Beechcraft "Princess" to assure that this "oldster" didn't bend the "Princess." I told the young pilot who was riding in the right seat some of my experiences during the Korean War. That young man didn't know where Korea was.

FINIS, SEMPER FI

The Vought F4U "Corsair"

Photo courtesy of Squadron/Signal Productions

Dimensions

Wingspan	41 ft.
Length	33 ft. 8 in.
Height	16 ft. 1 in.

Weights

Empty	9,205 lb.
Gross	12,420 lb.
Maximum Takeoff	14,670 lb.

Performance

Maximum Speed	446 mph at 26,200 ft.
Service Ceiling	41,500 ft.
Maximum Range	1,560 mi.

Power Plant

Pratt-Whitney R-2800 eighteen-cylinder radial engine, developing 2,100 hp for takeoff and 2,450 hp maximum

Armament

Six 0.50 cal Colt-Browning M2 machine guns (some variants had four 20 mm cannons) and either two 1,000 lb bombs or eight 5 in. rockets

Glossary

APC Tablet: An old navy medical panacea, containing aspirin and codeine

BAR: Browning Automatic Rifle

Cactus Air Force: The nickname of the Guadalcanal polyglot air force in 1942

CG: Commanding General

Collateral Duties: Any assignment outside the scope of one's basic job, such as doing reports or helping the United Way.

Corsair: F4U type of marine fighter aircraft, "bent wing bird," terror of the Jap Zero

CVE: aircraft carrier- escort

Fly One: Controller of flight operations on an aircraft carrier

Fox Flag: The red and white code flag flown during flight operations

G-1: Marine staff section responsible for personnel

KMAAG: Korean Military American Advisory Group that trained some Koreans

MAG: Marine Aircraft Group

MCAB: Marine Corps Air Base

MCAS: Marine Corps Air Station

MP: manifold pressure within the cylinders of aircraft engines

NCO: non-commissioned officer, ranging from corporal to sergeant major

NKPA: North Korean People's Army

OGPU: Soviet secret police from 1922 to 1935.

Pogue: Distasteful title for anyone disliked by a combat marine, origin unknown

POW: Prisoner of War

Radio Shack: Ship's communication center

RECCE: Road Reconnaissance Mission

RESCAP: Rescue combat air patrol

Roger Pass: Perfect carrier landing

ROK: Republic of Korea (South Korea)

VMF: Marine fighter squadron

About John J. Fischer

John J. Fischer is a fourth generation Texan, born in Austin, Texas, and raised in the semi-Wild West environment of Central Texas. After more than two decades in the U. S. Marine Corps, a period that encompassed World War II, the Korean Conflict, the Bay of Pigs, and the onset of the Vietnam debacle, he retired from the military.

During his retirement, he entered the corporate world and also became a certified flight instructor. His business career ended in 1981. His flight instructor career ceased in 1993 at age seventy-one by way of an EKG that was a lot less than perfect. When his flying ended after almost sixty years, he had logged almost 23,000 hours.

His writing career began after a visit from an old and dear friend from U. S. Marine Corps days. They spent the evening relating some of those war stories that are often enhanced by several after-dinner brandies. His children listened, and then insisted that he put these stories on paper.

This is his second book of the Korean War. It is hoped that others will follow before memory fades.

He extends his gratitude to his wife of fifty-seven years for her patience when the word processor begins to make those clicking noises at 0300 when he finds it necessary to put a newly remembered flashback on paper before he forgets it.

About James V. Lee

James V. Lee writes and publishes true accounts that capture the essence of Americans in seldom-told stories. The founder of Salado Press, Lee wrote and self-published *Nine Years In The Saddle* (NYITS) in 1998 and assisted in writing *When Surrender Was Not An Option,* a WWII account (2002). Also in 2002, he published *Bridezilla,* a guide to wedding etiquette, for authors Noe Spaemme and Jeanne Hamilton. It was this success that led to Lee's involvement with *Escape From Korea.* While signing NYITS in Austin, Lee met John Fischer who also had a story worth telling–the result was *Escape From Korea.* Lee shines in his mission to assist in the creation of highly interesting and entertaining true stories about the lives of those caught up in significant and historical events, such as The Great Depression, WWII, and the Korean War.

Born near O'Donnell, Texas, in 1926, James V. Lee holds a bachelor's degree in English from Abilene Christian College (now University) and a master's degree in Education from Southwest Texas State University (now Texas State University, San Marcos). Lee is married and has two adult children. His interests include traveling, writing, physical fitness and nutrition, and gardening.